THE
CONSCIOUS
ENNEAGRAM

THE
CONSCIOUS
ENNEAGRAM

How to Move from
Typology to Transformation

ABI ROBINS

BROADLEAF BOOKS
MINNEAPOLIS

Cover art: Sarah Duet
Cover image: enjoynz/istock
Cover design: James Kegley

Print ISBN: 978-1-5064-6502-9
eBook ISBN: 978-1-5064-6503-6

Printed in Canada

FOR JUNIPER AND FARREN,
MAY THIS WORK MAKE THE WORLD
A BETTER PLACE FOR YOU TO GROW UP.

CONTENTS

CONTENTS

FOREWORD

The Enneagram isn't the first thing; it's the second thing. Abi instinctively understands this. They understand that the first thing is our life and lived experience. In order to survive as a human, we come hardwired for both present-centered *aliveness* and struggle. We are equipped with protective mechanisms like patterns of judgment, addictive desires, behaviors, and anxious reactions. Abi understands that these defenses limit our capacity for resilience along with grounded, genuine *aliveness* when we remain on automatic pilot.

PRACTICE

They are also unflinchingly honest in laying out what spiritual teacher George Gurdjieff calls "intentional suffering" where we consciously engage practice in order to awaken to these patterns. We all know the familiar feelings of a need for approval and connection or the need for power and control or the need for safety and security. The moment you decide to engage in a practice, you'll begin to understand *why* they worked in the first place. It's no small thing for an Enneagram 8 to approach things with openness and innocence and to come fresh to each moment holding paradoxical truths. Their entire self-system is setting off alarm bells, saying, "Warning, this is dangerous territory. Defend. Now." Or if a 2 begins to relax into their own repressed needs, the amygdala in the brain gets hijacked, and what surfaces is the existential anxiety that "I will lose connection."

As I write, we are experiencing a worldwide pandemic that has pulled back the veils on individual, relational, and communal suffering. We are feeling a collective loss of connection, control, and security. Our Enneagram patterns are designed to offer protection, and in these times, they are in full throttle. Furthermore, the collective field is activated, which impacts you and me. It's intense out there, and in comes Abi. They don't make empty promises of enlightenment in three days by reading this book, nor do they grandiosely try to convince us that they've arrived at the pinnacle of awakening and a life of bliss. (Amen and amen to that.) Rather, they walk the path of student and teacher.

They invite us into our own experience with their suggestions rather than one-size-fits-all prescriptions. Abi invites you to adjust and test out the practices for yourself yet clearly states the core truth that we may miss when we first become enamored of the power of the Enneagram, which is the second thing: we need to have a practice of witnessing our habits, accepting their function and their adherence to a practice. Otherwise, the Enneagram is simply another cognitive personality tool that offers fascinating information but little possibility of transformation. Knowledge of this powerful system is not enough. Enneagram memes are fun *entertainment*, learning about the Enneagram is interesting *education*, but practice offers the *transformation* of the passions of our type structure and ultimately our lives, relationships, and communities.

Abi also offers a practical reason for practice when they write, "Practice does not prevent; practice prepares." It prepares us for the day-to-day challenges of being human on this planet. Your practice gives you some handles when the pressure is on.

GUIDANCE AND LINEAGE
• •

When I first came across Abi's Instagram feed, I had a sense that this is someone who isn't putting out Enneagram memes for entertainment. They clearly had a knowledge of this powerful system, but more obviously, they were clearly doing the inner and outer work of transformation as they supported others on the path.

In spiritual work, the boomer generation has had the tendency to hyperindividualize our practice. There's an unconscious belief that "If it's to be, it's up to me." I have to go it alone, the proof will be my enlightenment, and I need to push anything that looks to be its opposite out of my awareness. This leads to excessive self-criticism if we stumble and much time and energy wasted on questions like "How come I have to go through this same thing yet *again*?"

We need a guide. The Institute of Noetic Science did exhaustive research on this question: How do people change and sustain that change? They interviewed hundreds of people and discovered four qualities of lasting change: attention, intention, *guidance*, and repetition (practice).

A solid guide (teacher/facilitator/coach/therapist) is grounded in a lineage and roots. In their book, Abi expands on why lineage matters and why the model has lasted hundreds of years. Abi spells out their guides, their lineage, and why it has mattered.

Yet the boomer style of hyperindividualization and an exhausting pursuit of perfection led to an overelevation of gurus, spiritual teachers, and clergy. These guides were often idealized as enlightened or as virtuous and pure. Some have not been held accountable for behaviors out of alignment with the very principles they teach. Guides have also had a tendency to hold themselves to a standard that doesn't honor their humanity, which pushes human foibles and frailties to shadow. Eventually, these frailties and foibles erupt as shadow behaviors that cause lasting damage. We've heard the stories and sustained the damage, and it's rattled many to the core.

Abi busts this illusion of their perfection at the gate. They're honest about their struggles, which gives space for you to be honest about yours. They're a few steps ahead on the trail because of their commitment practice, so they know some of the familiar stumbling blocks. They give you some solid perspective on what you might experience on the path. This is a different quality of guidance. It's one of authentic humility rather than pseudohumility (which is a construct of prideful self-importance). Authentic humility comes from the Latin word meaning "low, on the ground in the soil," and in spiritual practice, this means "I'm with you, sib. This stuff's hard. We're in it together." This is Abi. Abi's a voice of their generation saying, "Welcome to the human race. I'm not going to try to sell you on some illusion that I don't struggle too. Practice helps, but life still can knock me to my knees." It's one of the first things I noticed about them. It also points to Abi's grounding in a lineage that knows the limits of the human condition.

COMMUNITY
• •

Another pitfall of my generation's hyperindividualization of practice was that we lost our way somewhere between the 1960s/1970s era of social change and the 1980s era of acquisition and individualism. While experience has taught me the imperative of an individual practice as "I can't do as much good in the outer world if I don't attend to my inner life and transformation," I have also learned that the outer world shapes me *and* I shape it through my engagement with it. In these times of pandemic, climate crisis, and the largest civil rights movement in US history, we are seeing the perils of overemphasis on individualization. We need community.

Abi highlights the reality that we live and breathe in a world of relationship and community. I've been part of an Enneagram learning community for over eighteen years. We're doing life with awareness and intention, and I've watched people grow. I lead with the social type 7. I've experienced myself as being able to increase my capacity for presence when pain, limitations, and boredom set in because I've had the support of an honest, intentional, and compassionate community of *practice.* They've helped me with nuances like the ways in which my passion and sacrifice for community is another way to avoid pain. They bust my projections, which I might never see if I were sitting home alone in my practice and meditation chair.

Abi's three-legged stool identifies community as an imperative. I couldn't agree more. They extend this communal focus to social change in the world however we may be called to contribute. Each time I see them highlighting this on social media, my heart sings. We can't afford to close our eyes to the world unfolding. Furthermore, Abi's engagement with community has brought them face-to-face with their own shadow.

This is the gift and heartache of *community*. We see the truth of ourselves and others. Abi writes,

> Being able to differentiate between the normal and healthy (depending on how we respond to it) friction inherent in community and the abusive interactions we can have when our community is in disarray or downright dysfunctional and toxic is one of the most important skills we can develop on our journey of personal and/or spiritual growth. Again, there is no clear-cut checklist for this sort of thing, but as people familiar with the Enneagram, we can see how our types illuminate the subject for us. Whenever we are feeling friction that is directly related to our type, there's a good chance that this is something we can work with and work through. Each of the types might be more likely to throw in the towel over different kinds of friction. Yet if approached with care and compassion, these experiences could actually be transformative individually and collectively.

Practice brings us home to ourselves to face the truth, and the *guide* in the lineage offers the signposts that we're not the first to have walked this trail. Abi's a worthy guide to walk it with you.

Leslie Hershberger

INTRODUCTION

THE THREE - LEGGED STOOL

"You're such an 8!"

"What the f**k is that supposed to mean?!" I retorted
dismissively in my typically crass manner.

Some friends and I were cooking our weekly postyoga
dinner. The conversation had gotten heated and somewhat
tense as a more tentative friend described being unsure of
her next career move. I had little patience for indecision and
felt that if she wanted something, she should just *do* it already. I was passionately making my point when my new
bestie Matthias piped up with his number comment. Then
he continued, "It means you want to push other people. You
need to be against. And you enjoy arguing with people."

"Well, yeah, but I only do it for their own good!" I said.

The room went quiet. Matthias and our other friends
looked expectantly at me as if they wanted me to catch up
and see what they all already knew. Then it clicked for me:
I had just done exactly what he said I would.

We all had a good laugh as I conceded Matthias's point. I
didn't want to seem too interested in the moment—you know,

I had to play it cool—but I was very intrigued. How did he know so much about me? I was new in town, and while I felt a strong connection to my newfound friends, we had really only known each other for a few weeks. I wanted to know what he knew. So a few days later, Matthias and I had coffee, and he told me all about this thing called the Enneagram.

I was certainly skeptical as Matthias shared with me all about this tool that was somehow both ancient and modern, Christian and connected to Sufi traditions and kabbalah, simple yet deep and nuanced; it seemed too good to be true. But I wasn't about to turn my nose up at something that could give me a leg up. I desperately needed one. I had crash-landed a few months earlier when my life completely fell apart. I went from living with the man I wanted to marry, in a city I loved, building a blossoming music career, and working a day job that was meaningful and fulfilling to being single and un-employed, living with my grandmother in a small town in Arkansas, and having my new record flop, all in the span of about three months. Oh, and did I mention that in the midst of all this, I realized that I was queer? To put it gently, things in my life had suddenly become really hard. As much as I hated to admit it, I needed help. And a lot of it.

The more Matthias spoke, the faster my skepticism faded. "8s are independent, don't like accepting help, and fear being betrayed."

Check, check, and . . . yes, check. It was all true for me, and suddenly I began to see the ways my Enneagram type had played into my current situation. Accepting help was new for me. The twenty-five years leading up to this time in my life had been marked by a fierce independence and a strong sense that I could do anything I set my mind to. These aren't bad characteristics on their own, but more than just feeling as if I was *capable* of going at things alone, I felt I *had* to, that I couldn't trust anyone to be there for me or back me up when I needed them. And it didn't help that I had more than a few scars to reinforce that belief. This was how I approached everything in my life. With my music career, I threw myself headfirst into booking my own shows and tours and writing and producing my own records. I became an industry unto myself. And while I loved helping other artists along the way, I made sure I was always the one in charge for fear of losing control of it all. This same fervor played out in my closest friendships and my intimate relationship. I would be all in from day one, using my intensity and authenticity as a diversion from real intimacy and vulnerability, and to tell the truth, this approach worked pretty well, until all of a sudden, it didn't.

"8s use denial to avoid their softer feelings. They don't want to admit how things affect them. They think if they just keep pushing, they'll be invincible," Matthias continued.

I could feel my heart sink with each word. My relationship had been failing for some time, and while neither my boyfriend nor I knew the real reason (I, at this point, had no clue I was queer), I knew "our problems" were really "my problems," so I ended it. After our breakup, I tried to keep moving through the world the way I always had, but things only got more difficult. It seemed as though the harder I tried to make my usual way of life work again, the worse things got. I just kept pushing, though, because I didn't know what else to do. I pushed and pushed until I pushed myself into filing for bankruptcy and spending a day in county jail. Definitely not a good look.

Matthias and I finished our coffee and conversation, and he suggested some places to look for more learning. As he left, I pulled out my laptop and ordered a couple of books he recommended. I was still unsure about this strange-looking symbol, but I was ready for things to change. I had hit rock bottom. I didn't know why things weren't working for me the way they used to, and I had even less of an idea of how to do anything different. I was utterly lost and confused.

So imagine my surprise when I opened up a book and saw all my problems written out in black and white.

WHAT IS THE ENNEAGRAM, ANYWAY?

The Enneagram is a powerful and complete tool for detailing the intricate system known as the human personality. A brilliant blend of Western psychology and Eastern spirituality, it allows us to look beyond our patterned behavior or indiscriminate likes and dislikes to our deepest desires and motivations. It clearly maps nine distinct styles or types of personalities in vivid high definition, taking into account the shifts, nuances, and flexibility that are innate to the human experience. It allows us to see not just our strengths and the parts of ourselves we are willing to show to the world but also our weaknesses and the parts of ourselves that our ego has dedicated itself to keeping hidden. The Enneagram can predict with stunning accuracy the struggles we will face while we are in this world: the recurring issues in our relationships, the conflicts and turbulence in our careers, and the battles we face with our connection to the divine. They're there as plain as the words on this page for all to see.

The Enneagram shows us clearly where we are *and* where we could be. All of our darkest pain seems intricately tied to all of the truly magical parts of ourselves and what we have to offer the world. If there is a patterned way of relating to those we love that has caused harm, recognizing the pattern provides an opportunity to change and find healing. The Enneagram shows us all the ways we engage with the world that cause us pain and suffering, and it also shows us that we already have what we need to be free from this suffering. It is this breadth that makes the Enneagram utterly captivating to so many.

This was certainly my experience as I immersed myself in the books Matthias recommended to me. It was both a relief and a hard callout. I felt exposed but at the same time comforted, as if everything was saying, "Yes, things are bad, and it actually *is* your fault, but it's OK. Things will get better." With this newfound information and insight into my own inner workings, I was able to really turn my life around. As I look back on the last decade of my life, discovering the Enneagram was a clear turning point. In some sense, I can divide my life into two large sections of time: BE (before Enneagram) and AE (after Enneagram).

WHAT DOES THE ENNEAGRAM OFFER US?

When I started working with the Enneagram, my life blossomed. Sure, when I found it, there really wasn't anywhere to go but up. Even still, my life has continued to grow and change and develop and improve past what I had ever thought possible for myself. Through working with this tool, I've learned how to slow down and not push myself so hard. I've developed the capacity for true intimacy and have learned to embrace the gentler and more sensitive sides of myself. I've also learned how to take responsibility for myself and my actions, owning up to how I've caused harm to others and learning how to make things right. These skills and capacities have completely transformed my life, my relationships, how I see the world, and my connection to the divine.

Essentially, by having a better understanding of myself and what drives my behavior, I've been able to develop more self-awareness and self-compassion. These two qualities have allowed me to fully lean into my patterns when my gifts are called for, slow myself down and choose something different when they're not, and be kind and compassionate to myself when I get the two confused. The Enneagram gave me the map I needed to move forward in my spiritual journey. By learning more about the other people in my life, I've developed a better understanding of their particular struggles and can better support them in their journeys as well. The Enneagram has shown me this work is never over, and there is always room to be astonished by what's possible.

From what I can tell, the Enneagram's greatest gift to us is growth—and not growth in the capitalistic, productivity-metric sense, but growth more in the sense of thriving and flourishing. This tool allowed me to grow in such a way that I've dedicated my life to sharing it with others and helping them experience the same kind of growth. Like most people who've found something that's drastically reshaped their lives, I wanted to tell everyone I could about this amazing tool. I had become a full-fledged Ennea-evangelist! As I became more and more involved in spreading the good word of the Enneagram, though, I started to notice that not everyone shared my excitement for this tool. I was shocked to hear stories of people who didn't find the same kind of growth and freedom I did and even more shocked to hear that many people had written the Enneagram off as just some new woo-woo replacement for astrology. I was baffled. Why didn't everyone experience this growth? Was I just some sort of anomaly?

WHY DOESN'T THE ENNEAGRAM WORK FOR EVERYONE?

The Enneagram is a deeply powerful tool for personal and communal transformation. The last fifty years have seen an immense development of the Enneagram as a system, covering everything from psychological defense mechanisms to spiritual gifts, childhood wounds to neuroscience, somatic experiences to team dynamics. It's clear there is no better system for understanding our patterned behavior and what we are inherently capable of. The one thing missing from this immense lexicon of information, though, is the *how*. The Enneagram does not have a *method of application*. And it should be clarified that this is not merely an issue within one particular school of Enneagram training. All major schools and teachers agree: this information is not enough—but they don't give much more than that. Without an understanding of *how* to use this information, the kind of growth and transformation I experienced is hard to find.

Many teachers have highlighted this gap in the Enneagram as positive, explaining that because it doesn't have a specified method of application, it can be used anywhere. Corporate team building, relationships, business marketing, parenting, spiritual enlightenment: the sky is the limit! While I believe one of the Enneagram's strongest assets is its versatility, if there's no basic framework of how to integrate this information into one's life, the Enneagram may reach multitudes but change very few. At best it becomes ineffectual, and at worst it becomes a tool that reinforces the very patterns it seeks to free us from. The Enneagram is reaching more and more people every day, but this gap has left us to our own devices when it comes to the journey from where we are to where we could be.

As I came to understand this gap better, I started to look more closely at the circumstances of my life that I also attributed to my immense personal growth. I started chatting with others who *had* experienced growth with the Enneagram and what it had looked like for them. There were some striking similarities in our stories, and I started to see some clear and predictable patterns.

From these patterns, I began piecing together what I believe to be the next pillar of the Enneagram canon, a method of application that allows people to really put this information to work in their lives. And that's what this book is about: not the what, but the *how*. This book is focused on the *how* of actually putting the system to work. This method draws from my experience and training as a yoga therapist, my time studying the Gurdjieff work—which the Enneagram is rooted in, my personal experiences, and the experiences of others who've undergone real transformation through using the Enneagram. This method adds a much-needed structure to the path of personal development without sacrificing the universality that allows the Enneagram to be so far-reaching and powerful.

NEW TO THE ENNEAGRAM?

As I mentioned, the focus in this book is not so much on the *what* of the Enneagram but on the *how*. This means that we'll be starting off with the assumption that you have a little Ennea-knowledge under your belt. If this is the case, go ahead and dive in. I think you'll be both inspired and challenged by the content of this book. That being said, it would be foolish of me to assume that everyone reading this book already has a foundational and functional understanding of the Enneagram. If you're in need of an Enneagram 101, I'm certainly not going to leave you hanging. You can flip to the back of the book and read through the appendix. There I present my personal approach to the Enneagram, the concepts and theories I've found most helpful, as well as basic descriptions of the types and the system as a whole. This will allow even the most Ennea-illiterate to move through the pages of this book with all of the tools and understanding they need, and it also serves as a way to calibrate the Ennea-experts to my way of looking at and working with the system. Context is everything, and understanding how I approach the system will undoubtedly support you in working out how to apply it.

THE THREE-LEGGED STOOL

• •

When I look back at the wreckage that was my life just a few years ago, I credit three things aside from the Enneagram with getting me out of the deep existential hole I was in. The first was yoga. I still find this somewhat hard to wrap my mind around because I used to hate yoga. I had no interest in it. I had tried it a few times and failed utterly due to my tight hamstrings and extreme aversion to looking like a fool in public. The only reason I went to a yoga class while I was in Arkansas was because I had a crush on my coworker, who said she would also be attending. That crush never went anywhere, but as it turns out, I didn't hate that yoga class. In fact, I maybe even liked it. I certainly liked how I felt afterward—so much so that I decided to go again the next week, and the next, and pretty soon I was in the studio as often as the teacher would let me in. It became the way I started my day, moving, breathing, and meditating. It opened me up in ways I never knew were possible. It became a place where I could work through the things I was facing in my life, but on a level deeper than I can really describe. Yoga affected me deeply. In short, yoga was a *practice* for me, and that practice became a place of immense personal and spiritual healing.

In the midst of developing my personal yoga practice, I started to build some deeply meaningful one-on-one relationships with people who were able to offer me sound guidance and support. The first was with my therapist. Starting therapy was a godsend, and I wouldn't have been able to move through the challenges I faced while at my rock bottom without it. Just as important as my therapist, though,

were my teachers: the women who guided me in my practice and taught me what they knew about both yoga and life.
Through them I felt connected to something bigger than
myself. Something that was flowing through them was now
flowing through me and leading me toward the next steps
in my life. I was a part of a *lineage*. This lineage encouraged
me and put my story into a larger context. Things started
making more sense and seemed less daunting as I learned of
others in this line of spiritual teachers who had already encountered the challenges I was now facing.

While my newfound practice and lineage both drastically changed my life in profound ways, I know I would have
never made it out of the mess of my life without the friends
and *community* that surrounded me during that dark time.
These people took me in; they supported me, they pushed
me, they cheered me on. We did life together in a way I had
never experienced before. Hardly a day went by where we
didn't see each other, and if we didn't cross paths physically,
we would be chatting it up in a group text, planning our next
get-together. These people saw me at my worst, crying and
drunk in the backseats of their cars as they drove me home,
but they also saw me at my best, making decisions to take responsibility for my actions and move my life forward. These
people were invested in my growth but also deeply invested
in their own. I got to see them in the dark and the light just
like they saw me, and we were all able to move through life
with more grace because of it.

As I've listened to others tell me about the growth they've
experienced with the Enneagram, the same themes are always present, even if they can't name them explicitly. Even as
I look at how Gurdjieff, the man responsible for introducing

the Enneagram to the West, taught and ran his school of personal development, the elements are there. It's clear to me now that there are three crucial elements all humans need for their personal development: a practice, or a way to "try on" the teachings in a way that easily translates to real life; a lineage, or a teacher who can connect us to the heart of the teachings and show us how to connect to our own hearts; and a community, or more specifically, a group of people who are also committed to this work whom we can interact with regularly.

Many Enneagram teachers in the last several years have caught on to the idea of a personal practice and its importance in our personal and spiritual development. Others have been adamant in their focus on building communities around this work, while still others are clear that the key is to build a relationship with a qualified teacher. Because of both my personal experience and my time spent with the Gurdjieff work, I have come to see that the real key lies not with any one of these three things alone but in developing each of them and bringing them into balance in your life. I see each one of these elements—practice, lineage, and community— as a leg of a stool. In order for the stool to be sturdy and functional, all three legs must be strong and balanced, or else it will topple over. Now, I should make it clear that this is not any sort of completely new idea. The Buddhists have had the concept of "Buddha, Dharma, Sangha" (loosely translated to "teacher, work [or practice], community") for hundreds of years, and many other spiritual traditions have had these elements at their core, even if they weren't explicitly written out. It is important in the further development of the relatively young system of the Enneagram of personality, though, that we make these connections explicit in order to clarify and solidify the practical application of this teaching.

If you're sincere in your study of the Enneagram, I would expect that you have already developed at least one of these three legs out of sheer instinct. As we begin our journey into personal and spiritual growth, one of these legs will seem obvious, as all people and types will lean into one aspect and may focus on it exclusively. This often causes an extreme leap in personal development. The trouble is that this leap is almost always followed by a stalling or plateau that then leads to regression, leaving people not much better off than when they started. It's this vicious cycle that has left many Enneagram-hopefuls feeling disillusioned and discontent. Can you imagine trying to reach the fruit at the top of a tree with a pogo stick? That is essentially what's happening when we rely solely on one leg of the personal growth stool. We need all three legs in order to maintain balance and help us reach our full potential through the growth the Enneagram offers us.

SO WHAT DOES GROWTH LOOK LIKE, ANYWAY?

This approach to applying Enneagram information is powerful and effective regardless of your particular understanding of the system. It doesn't matter if you learned it from Helen Palmer or Russ Hudson or your next-door neighbor; this application will help you make the information work in your life. When this happens, things will inevitably start to change, but how will you know if they're changing in the right ways? Being clear about what this change and growth looks like from an Enneagram perspective is vital in making sure we're staying on the right path.

A very popular saying floats around the community to the tune of "As you grow, you will look less and less like your type," and while I agree to some extent, real growth is more about having the ability to respond consciously to the situations life presents you with. In some cases, the situation will require you to use the gifts of your type, while other situations may call for something you're not particularly skilled at. Our types are rigid, stiff, and only offer us a small amount of unconscious, habitual behaviors, so it would stand to reason that real, meaningful, and tangible growth *is more about becoming conscious and aware of our behaviors and being able to choose different ones when necessary* than it is about eradicating our type structures.

As you begin to apply the principles from this book in your life, it's these abilities of flexibility and conscious response that you will want to keep an eye out for. They may not look the way you anticipated, and I can almost guarantee they won't feel the way you expect (or want) them to, but these will be signs that you're on the right track. They will most likely show up in unexpected places. If you're focused on growing spiritually, you may see these signs pop up in your work life; if you're working on relational issues, you may start to experience an opening spiritually. This doesn't mean that anything is going wrong; it's your reminder that all of these things are connected. Gurdjieff called his students to work as "householders," meaning everything—every aspect of our lives—is fair game for growth, and we can and will experience these higher states of consciousness in all areas of our lives. Honestly, I can't think of anything more exciting.

MOVING FORWARD

As you move through this book, I encourage you to not take anything I say as gospel. Please try it on and see how it works for you. There may be pieces that fit like a glove, and there may be others that feel like a pair of shoes two sizes too big. You may not resonate with every word right now—or ever—and that's OK. I hope that this book is something that you can come back to over the years as your journey shifts and changes, like a trusty field guide for navigating your inner landscape. I'm confident that no matter where you are on your personal or spiritual journey with the Enneagram, there will be something in here for you that helps you move forward, thrive, and flourish.

LEG 1

PRACTICE

CHAPTER 1
WHAT MAKES A PRACTICE?

I remember right where I was sitting, on the floor in the corner of the green yoga studio in Austin, Texas, when my teacher at the time, Mark Uridel, said these words to the class: "We are what we do most." I was shocked into attention as Mark explained how the movements we make each day shape our bodies. Quite literally, if we sit all day, our bodies become sitting bodies: our hip flexors will be short and tight, our lower backs will be rounded and often in pain, our glutes will be weak and overly long. If we run ten miles every day, our bodies become running bodies: strong calves and quadriceps, tight hamstrings, tense shoulders and upper backs. In an attempt to be as efficient as possible—or in other words, use the least amount of energy possible to complete a task—our bodies literally change the way they function physiologically as well as reshape themselves physically. The human body is dynamic and highly intelligent; it will adapt intuitively to be the best equipped for the situations it faces most often. What can be said about the body in this case also applies to the mental and emotional aspects of our experiences. If we experience anger often, we will turn ourselves into angry people; if we're always thinking of how things might go wrong, we will become worried, anxious people. This is the basis of the phrase "practice makes permanent." What I love most about what I was learning in class that day, though, is how clearly it illustrates our tendency to find our identities in the things we think, feel, and do.

When we move in certain ways repeatedly, think the same thoughts over and over, or have the same habitual emotional reactions, not only are we shaping how our bodies, minds, and hearts function; we are also shaping how we see ourselves and how we will inevitably train the world to see us. This is our Enneagram type. Whether a tendency or temperament is inborn or we develop our types in response to our early childhood experiences or some combination of the two, what is clear is that at some point in our young lives, we all found the ways of thinking, feeling, and doing that got us what we wanted. Then we started thinking, feeling, and doing those same things over and over again. This caused our systems to develop in a way that would make those thoughts, feelings, and actions easily accessible, and we started to see ourselves as the qualities they produced. This is often a great advantage to us early in life, as we are using strategies that have proven to be effective at getting us what we need. The problem is that the more we do something, the harder it is to do something else, and as we age, we often find that our patterns are far too limited to meet the demands of our lives in a meaningful and fulfilling way. If our entire system is built around being right, it will be extremely difficult for us to admit when we're wrong. If we are wholly identified with being the helpful friend, we won't be able to see the ways in which we need the help and support of others. Without the ability to admit when we're wrong or ask for help and support, our lives and development will be stunted, and we will miss out on the beauty and meaning that life has to offer.

Of the nine Enneagram personality types, I identify most with type 8. I have built an identity around being strong and capable, and all of my thoughts, feelings, and actions have functioned in ways that support this identity. This served me quite well throughout my life—until it didn't, as you read in the introduction. The problem for me has come most often in the form of relationships. I remember distinctly one night a partner asked me point-blank what I needed from her. While I can look back and see I was most definitely in need of support, at that time, my identity was all about how capable I was. I didn't need anyone's help. I didn't *need* anything from anyone; I could do it myself. So I responded with "Nothing." I remember the look of annoyance on her face as clear as day. Needless to say, that relationship didn't last long. As I engaged more with my inner work and started taking self-observation more seriously, I saw this pattern popping up in other relationships as well, with many of the same consequences. The more I did my own inner work, the more I didn't want to be saying "Nothing" when my partner asked me what I needed—but I didn't know what else to say. I had to learn to say something else. I had to practice first knowing what I actually felt and then putting words to it. Then I had to practice having access to all of that when I was asked. It was a lot of practicing, but now I have more to say than "Nothing," and my relationships are flourishing because of it.

So many of the people I've worked with have relayed similar experiences with seeing what's wrong but not knowing how to do anything else. It's infuriating to see that what you're doing isn't working but feeling as though you don't have any other options. This is why we need practices. In order to do something different from what we've always done, we can't just jump in the deep end and magically expect to be Olympic swimmers. We start in the baby pool, we get used to the water, then we might be able to go out to where we can't touch the bottom, and soon we're treading water, and then swimming like the pros (or at least well enough to get from one side of the pool to the other without having to call a lifeguard). I played sports my whole life and always heard the phrase "proper practice prevents poor performance." While the alliteration is a little over the top, the point is very powerful. If we want to choose something else when it really counts, we have to practice that "something else" when the pressure is off. This allows our systems to change slowly, over time, instead of demanding that they change all at once when we're in a fight with our spouse or coworker.

It's helpful to think of our hearts, heads, and bodies as a complex system of highways. If you want to go somewhere you've never been, or if you have the sense that there may be a faster way to get to where you want to go, you can't just hop the curb and start driving. You have to build new roads. Practice is the construction crew for these new roads. The process often feels slow, like the construction is never going to be over, but then one day, often unexpectedly, you'll find yourself cruising down a newly paved highway to a brand-new destination.

PRACTICE 101

• •

There are three main elements that must be present in order to call something a practice: attention, intention, and consistency. The first element may seem like the most obvious. If we are undertaking any sort of practice that allows us to be more present and open to what life is offering us, we need to be aware of what we're doing. We need to be present to what is happening. We need to give this activity our *attention*. Our attention is a lot like our breath—it is always running whether we notice it or not—and we're always attentive to something. In Enneagram terms, each type has a Habit of Attention,* a place where our attention will always drift back to if left unchecked. From this Habit of Attention, we get accustomed to only seeing certain things, and those are usually the things we want to see in any given situation. What we need to develop is Conscious Attention. Conscious Attention is the ability to keep yourself focused on any single task or object while remaining relaxed. The best way to gauge how relaxed you are is to notice your breath; relaxed breathing is both smooth and long. If your breathing is tense and shallow, even though you may be intently focusing on a task or job, you aren't using Conscious Attention. Likewise, if your breath is smooth and long but your attention is jumping from thing to thing, you are not using Conscious Attention. Any activity, be it walking, praying, or doing a crossword puzzle, could be considered a practice if you can bring your Conscious Attention to it.

A dear friend of mine walks a labyrinth every morning before he starts his day. In times of great distress, he picks up

---

* You can read more about the Habit of Attention in the appendix.

a rock, holds it in his hand as he walks, and pours his prayers into it. To any outside observer, he is just a man walking in circles with a fistful of rocks, but his attention is fully in his walking, fully in his prayers, and fully in the rocks he carries. His breath stays smooth and long as he breathes life into the rocks in his hands. It's his attention that makes these actions a practice, and it's a practice that benefits him and those he loves. I've had the opportunity to hold several of those rocks in my hands after they traveled the labyrinth with him, and they are no ordinary rocks. You can feel the warmth and love that have been poured into them long after his practice has finished. Their journey around the labyrinth changed them, all because of his Conscious Attention.

After attention comes *intention*. There are plenty of moments where we may fall into Conscious Attention without really trying. These are beautiful moments of presence that come to us as gifts from the divine, but these moments could hardly be considered a practice. That's because there is no *intention* behind them. Intention is a powerful force, and when we make clear our intentions, we are much more likely to actually move in their direction. For moments of Conscious Attention to become a practice, we must be intentional about practicing them. Without a clear and expressed intention to practice something new, we will undoubtedly end up right back in our patterns. Many clients I work with accomplish this by having a set time in their day to practice or maybe even a special area in their house, apartment, or bedroom that they use only for their practice. These actions are symbols of their intention and make their practice more effective. Not only is it important to have the intention to practice; we must also be intentional about what we're practicing. If we want to move ourselves out of our habitual responses to life, we must be intentional about taking time to practice something different. Just showing up on our yoga mat, meditation cushion, or prayer labyrinth and intentionally practicing won't help us long-term if we're practicing things that only reinforce our patterns.

I practiced hot yoga for years. I was intentional about creating time in my life and schedule to make it to classes where I was focused and breathing, but after a while I noticed that I was pushing myself harder and harder. It soon became clear to me that I was "practicing" something that wasn't actually a practice for someone who leads with type 8. I was feeding off the intensity instead of learning how to become aware of the subtlety of my body and breath. So often our practices end up doing more harm than good because we aren't *intentional* enough about what we are practicing and how it's affecting us. Don't worry, though! There is more on how to avoid these practice pitfalls in chapter 4.

The last piece of the puzzle for developing a practice is consistency. They say it's "practice, practice, practice" that gets you to Carnegie Hall, not just one "practice." Could you imagine picking up a guitar for the first time, practicing intently for thirty minutes, and then getting up to perform in front of thousands of people? That's a particular kind of nightmare because we all know that in order to become proficient at anything, it takes repeated and *consistent* practice. You might have the intention to practice and bring your Conscious Attention to a task, but if you only ever do it once, its effects will be short-lived. I think of these moments more like a personal Conscious Experiment instead of a Conscious Practice. I might like the way the experiment ends up, or I may not, but I haven't committed myself to it as a practice yet. When we commit to consistent practice, the effects of the practice and the experience of it in the moment deepen as our system starts to organize itself around these new qualities. Like my yoga teacher said, "We are what we do most." So if we want to change, we need to practice consistently.

Writing a book is very hard. In the beginning of writing this book, I was only writing when I could block out a large chunk of time. I would write in the morning or at night or in the middle of the afternoon, often for several hours at a time, but I could only do that a couple of times a week. I've always enjoyed writing and considered myself a strong writer, but something about this process called all of that into question. I always felt frazzled, and I didn't like what I wrote. Eventually my mentor suggested I set more parameters around when and how I wrote. She encouraged me to write more *consistently* even if I didn't write for very long. So I built some practices around my writing and started treating writing itself as a practice. I shifted my work schedule so that I could work out and then write each morning. Suddenly it felt more routine, and it felt as though my body, heart, and mind knew when it was time to write. Sure, there were still plenty of hard days, but in showing up more consistently to write, I was keeping a small promise to myself, and the writing slowly started to shift. Instead of trying to knock out four thousand words in a day and then being mentally and emotionally exhausted for the rest of the week, I focused on small chunks of writing and just staying in contact with the material each day. Each day's progress might not have looked that impressive on its own, but it was still effective. And look! Now you're reading this actual book!

It's also important to note that practicing consistently doesn't necessarily mean practicing every day, although that can be helpful for some practices. Some practices aren't meant to be daily rituals, but we can still practice them with consistency. Think of going to therapy or getting a massage—those can both be practices we show up to consistently, maybe once every two weeks or once a month, but I don't know anyone who has the time, money, or emotional fortitude to go to therapy or get a massage every day. Setting a consistent schedule for both of these, though, will make them more effective in your life. Your body, heart, and mind will all find a flow when there is a consistent rhythm to your practices.

ZOOM OUT

When these three elements are in place, we are practicing. When you're first building a practice, though, it's important to view your practice from thirty thousand feet. In other words, if your practice is about changing the big picture of your life, then you have to look at the big picture to judge its efficacy. If we are too zoomed in, each momentary wavering of attention, intention, or consistency will feel like a death knell for our practice. With more context, though, we can see that overall, these elements are in place. While there may be moments when our Conscious Attention slips, our intention is unclear, or we aren't showing up as consistently as we'd hope, the real key to success in any practice is to just come back to it. When you zoom out, it's easier to see these slips or misses in a larger context, and there they often have a lot less weight and a lot less shame. The remedy for any of these issues is simple: just start again. Have you missed your yoga class the last couple of weeks? Just start again today. Not sure why you're still setting your alarm for the crack of dawn? Maybe it's time to refresh your intention. Does your attention continue to wander to the day's to-do list during your meditation? Just gently bring it back. It is impossible to have all of these elements perfectly in place at all times, but that is exactly why they call it a practice. We're not meant to get it right 100 percent of the time. If we could, we obviously wouldn't need the practice.

DIFFERENT KINDS OF PRACTICE

Because almost any activity or task can be considered a practice, it can be daunting to know where to start. The Enneagram gives us a wonderful outline of the things in our lives we need to develop to be happy, healthy, and whole, but without an understanding of the different kinds of practices and how they affect us, we lack a clear direction. As a yoga therapist, I have studied practices from ancient spiritual traditions as well as modern science and health care. I've found that all valid and effective practices address three different elements, and understanding these aspects is instrumental in developing a practice that is consistent and effective.

The first elements our practice can address are content and capacity. As we work to develop our practices, it's helpful to understand how different practices affect different things within us. There are practices that work directly with the content of our thoughts, emotions, or physical body, such as the repetition of affirmations or denials to address a particular recurring thought pattern, the use of therapy to work through repressed emotions, or physical therapy to rehab a specific injury. Content practices are often much more personalized and specific because they are focused exactly on the content each person holds in their mind, heart, and body. They are also focused on the past, directly affecting the things we've acquired throughout our life. Many of these things we still carry with us even though they no longer serve us.

Capacity practices directly affect our ability to experience, contain, and fully process the situations of our lives mentally, emotionally, and physically. These are practices like Centering Prayer, which increases our ability to be unattached to our thoughts and experiences; Somatic Experiencing, which strengthens our capacity to hold difficult emotional experiences; or even weight training to increase our physical strength and ability to literally hold and carry more in a physical sense. Capacity practices focus on our future and what we're moving into. These practices can often be more generally applied because they deal less with the specific content of our hearts, minds, or bodies and are focused instead on increasing our tolerance for experience. Most practices can easily address issues of both content and capacity, but it is helpful to be clear about the specific intention of a practice at any given time, as the intention will make the practice more effective.

Another element of our practices to consider is if they are Via Negativa or Via Positiva—in other words, Are our practices building us up or tearing us down (in a good way)? Via Negativa practices are designed to empty our selves of the things that prevent us from experiencing our highest potential, while Via Positiva practices help align us with the things that move us toward that same goal. When dealing with our hearts, Centering Prayer—a form of Christian meditation designed to open our hearts to the divine—is considered a Via Negativa practice, while Meta meditation—also known as the Loving Kindness meditation—is a Via Positiva practice. From an intellectual perspective, practicing affirmations ("I am safe, I am secure, I am loved") would be considered a Via Positiva practice, whereas practicing denials ("I am not my thoughts, I am not alone, I am not afraid") would be considered Via Negativa. Addressing our physical capacities through Yin Yoga, where the goal is to surrender to the posture and let go of the need to control or manipulate the situation, would be a Via Negativa practice, while CrossFit, a high-intensity training focused on building strength and overall fitness, would be considered a Via Positiva practice. In general, Via Negativa practices give us the room and the freedom to develop ourselves, while Via Positiva practices move us toward the things we wish to embody. Just as with the idea of content/capacity, a single practice may have elements of both Via Positiva and Via Negativa, but it is important to use them each intentionally. Via Negativa practices are often used when first developing a practice in order to empty or at least loosen the old ways of operating to make room for what the Via Positiva practices seek to build within us.

The last element of practices that is important to define is which Center of Intelligence* they are affecting. Understanding which center or centers our practice is directly affecting

* More on the Centers of Intelligence in the appendix.

will help guide us in our journey toward balance physically, mentally, and emotionally. If our practice is focused only on one of our centers, we will undoubtedly become off-kilter. As I discussed in the introduction, our growth and development in terms of the Enneagram are about both developing and balancing all three of our centers. Working on solely one center is missing two-thirds of the work. I hear a lot of new Enneagram enthusiasts say things like "I'm a 4, so I'm working on being more embodied" (the 4's repressed center is their Body Center), which is wonderful, but if a 4's only focus is developing and building up their least accessed center without working to balance and develop their most used center or their support center, they won't experience the kind of growth they could otherwise. In the next chapter, I explore this concept of a three-centered practice in more depth while fully illustrating how the concepts of content/capacity and Via Negativa / Via Positiva play out in the real world.

PUTTING IT ALL TOGETHER

My goal is not to tell you exactly what and how you should practice based on your type. And honestly, you should run in the opposite direction from anyone who wants to do that. Even within our types, we are all infinitely different, and while there may be many similarities among people of the same type, there will be just as many differences. My teacher Chase Bossart says, "General practice, general results. Specific practice, specific results." The goal of this work is not to give you the general practices for your type so that you will only experience the general results of your work but to give you the pieces necessary for this work to take place and show you how to use them. This way you can create something specific to you, and you can experience the true growth and development that are meant for you. I will share examples of people who've engaged in different practices and what it's offered them in terms of growth in their type, but these are all people who found what worked for them. It's up to you to find what works for you.

CHAPTER 2

THREE - CENTERED PERSON, THREE - CENTERED PRACTICE

Piano was my first instrument. Seven-year-old me was so excited when my mother informed me that I was finally going to have lessons. I learned some scales and even performed "Jolly Old St. Nicholas" for a Christmas recital one year. A couple of years later, I transitioned to trumpet for the elementary school band (why they thought it would be a good idea to have elementary-schoolers in a band is anyone's guess). I had to learn new finger movements and how to buzz my lips, but I had a head start in reading music, and my ear had already developed into something that was somewhat useful. When I was ten, I bought myself my first guitar. *That's* when things got interesting. While I enjoyed both piano and trumpet, my love of music was set aflame once I started learning the guitar. I was mostly self-taught, but the musical foundation I had developed through learning piano and trumpet served me very well. At seventeen I started touring the country, playing shows wherever they would have me, hauling along six more instruments. By the time I retired as a musician about a decade later, I played upward of a dozen different instruments.

Other musicians might find this story familiar—once you learn one instrument, all the other instruments become a little easier to understand. This is because music is the same no matter what you're using to make it. The only difference is the techniques you use. This also applies to how we work with our Centers of Intelligence. As I develop my Body Center and work on different ways of moving and taking action in my life, my Heart Center slowly starts to open, and my Head Center starts to see new possibilities, and vice versa. Working with one center will make working in another center more accessible because the work of seeing, understanding, having compassion for, and letting go of our patterns is all the same in each center, we just use different techniques. Growth and transformation are the same regardless of what center they're happening in, but if we want to be proficient in all three, we have different techniques we need to master. Throughout this chapter, I'll discuss the different techniques for working with each of our centers as well as how we can use what we learn from one to affect the others.

Work on centers is twofold: we must make sure that our centers are balanced (that we have easy access to our Head, Heart, and Body Centers) and that each of our centers is fully developed. We might intuit that we should work to gain more access to our repressed center, which is very important, but it isn't the only piece. As I mentioned earlier, not only have we developed unconscious habits in how much access we have to each center (i.e., we access the dominant the most, the repressed the least, and the support center is recruited to help the dominant center), but each center has also developed its own unconscious habits of operation. So if we were only to bring up our repressed center but not loosen the habits, we would only have more access to an unconscious center, and our responses to the world around us wouldn't be much improved. The hope of engaging in these practices is that we will have equal access to all three centers and have the freedom to move consciously in each one.

THE BODY CENTER

When I first started practicing yoga, like most people who start a new exercise routine, I was mainly interested in changing my body. But over the course of about six months, something different was happening to me. I probably spent as much time crying in each heated power vinyasa class as I did sweating. I had *zero* clue what was going on, but each time I got up out of svasana, I felt different—better, even! I started having some important breakthroughs in therapy, and I was able to start and maintain a meditation practice for the first time. I was sitting still for what I think may have been the first time in my entire life. There was something about putting my body in all these new shapes and moving it in all these new ways that changed not only the way I was moving but also the ways I was thinking and experiencing my emotions. Working with my body opened the door to a whole new life.

The Body Center's particular skill sets are our kinesthetic abilities, physical sensations, and gut instincts or intuitive knowing. All of these are directly affected when we work with our Body Centers. Whether you have easy and ample access to these skills or very little, your Body Center has developed particular internally based habits of how you show up in the world. These internal habits also translate to external habits of movement. Do you hold your weight in the backs of your feet or in your toes? Do you favor your left leg when you walk or your right? While these external movement habits seem inconsequential, they can quickly add up to a body that is out of balance and unable to graciously meet the demands of our lives, and if our bodies are out of balance, our hearts and minds will be as well. Of course, balance in this instance doesn't just mean physical balance or symmetry; it has more to do with how easily our bodies are able to adapt to and flow with what life is presenting to us. There is ample room in this teaching for people of all body types and abilities. No matter what our bodies look or feel like, the way that we move (or don't move) directly affects the way that we think and feel. If you want to think and feel differently, you need to move differently, and this is where our Conscious Movement practice comes in.

WHAT IS A CONSCIOUS MOVEMENT PRACTICE?

Whether your practice is focused on opening and emptying yourself or building yourself up or focused on your body's content or capacity, what makes it truly powerful is your attention to sensation. Being able to feel what's happening in your body as it happens is what sets a Conscious Movement practice apart from other kinds of movement practices. Being able to sense your body and respond to it appropriately as it moves, stretches, and is challenged by new kinds of movements is also the number-one way to keep yourself safe from injury. As a yoga therapist, I've had many people come up to me and tell me about injuries they've sustained in their yoga classes. While I can sympathize, the truth is that it stopped being yoga the moment you asked your body to do something it wasn't ready for. It's the lack of attention to and trust in the body that leads to injury. While we must remain willing to be uncomfortable and may even be sore for a day or two after challenging our bodies in new ways, our practices should never cause pain. I've counseled many clients on the process of slowing down and taking it easy, as the "no pain, no gain" ethos has been programmed deep into our collective unconscious. As with all other spiritual practices, we should be replacing "no pain, no gain" with "slow and steady wins the race."

Our movement practices also need to be unpatterned, meaning we need to be moving in a way we don't normally move in everyday life. I obviously have an affinity for yoga and think it can be an excellent way to experience forms with your body that you wouldn't otherwise, but anticipating that this book will find its way into the hands of several very experienced yogis, I want to say that at some point, yoga asana often stops being a Conscious Movement practice. Once someone has "mastered" the movements and forms, there is a habit developed around them, meaning our attention can check out and we can go on autopilot as we go through our yoga class. For this reason, I often suggest other forms of movement to my clients who are experienced yogis: *tai chi*, Pilates, rock climbing, anything that is different from the habits they've developed in their yoga practice. What it all comes down to is moving in new ways. So even if you have an established workout or movement routine, your Conscious Movement practice may take you outside of it to move in ways your body hasn't experienced before.

In our movement practices, we can also work with the ideas of content/capacity as well as Via Negativa and Via Positiva. When we are working with the content of our Body Centers, we may be addressing an explicit physical movement issue, like the under- or overdevelopment of a certain muscle group, or physiological issues, like our digestion or how our immune system is functioning. Capacity in the Body Center has more to do with what our bodies are capable of and our strength, flexibility, physical balance, agility, cardiovascular health, and so on, all of which translate to our mental and emotional faculties as well. When looking at the ideas of Via Negativa / Via Positiva, we can ask ourselves, Is our practice emptying us and giving us more space, or is it building up something within us? Via Negativa practices develop flexibility or mobility in our bodies, giving us more space to move openly, like Yin Yoga, massage, or active release therapy. These are practices in which the focus is to let go. Via Positiva practices, on the other hand, develop our strength or stability in different areas, like weight training, running, or hatha yoga.

While the Body Center may be the most accessible center to begin our practices with, it is difficult to define what a healthy Body Center looks like according to the traditional Enneagram wisdom. In some ways, our Instinctual Drives* shift and balance as we work with our bodies, but there is

---

* More on the Instinctual Drives, or instincts, in the appendix.

also a more basic and fundamental way to define a healthy Body Center. Book 2, verse 46 of the Yoga Sutras states, स्थिरसुखमासनम्, or "*sthira sukham asanam.*" For those of you who are a little rusty with your Sanskrit, it means our posture should be both steady and at ease. While this sutra is telling us how we should go about our practices, I believe it is also a signpost for our journey toward growth in working with our bodies. As we develop our Body Centers, we will be steadier and more at ease in our physical bodies as well as in how we move throughout the world. As we develop more capacity in our bodies and work through the trauma stored in our tissues, we will experience a massive amount of freedom. We'll notice that both our mood and cognitive function will greatly improve, and we will feel better in our bodies. From this space, we will have more room to address the mental and emotional aspects of our lives.

THE HEART CENTER

I took my first real Enneagram class at my church in Austin fresh off another gnarly breakup (are y'all picking up on the pattern here?). It was in this class that I really came to grips with the fact that I was "feeling repressed." What this meant is that, as someone who leads with type 8, I had the least amount of access to my Heart Center. I could see this playing out in the aftermath of my recent breakup, as I simply wanted to "move on." I had little interest in dwelling on the feelings or emotions of the situation. As my classmates encouraged me to slow down enough to pay attention to what I was feeling, only one emotion came up: anger. I was mad as all get-out at how our relationship ended. The more the class pressed me, the more I realized I felt maybe three emotions: happy, sad, and angry (they didn't think "stoked" counted, though I still disagree). So I was assigned an emotions wheel (a circular emotional vocabulary list) to learn how to more accurately express how I was feeling. This assignment not only increased my emotional vocabulary; it helped me to pay more attention to what was happening to me emotionally. As I worked more explicitly with my Heart Center and slowly became more sensitive, something crazy started happening—I started developing more meaningful relationships. I felt more deeply connected to people, and when my now wife and I started dating, I could really *feel* that this was it for me.

This is what the Heart Center is all about: connection. We relate to other people through our Heart Center. Both the depth and health of our relationships are wholly dependent on how easily and consciously we can access this center. To start our work with our Heart Center, it's helpful to draw the line between content and capacity right off the bat and discuss practices for each separately. When the talk of the Heart Center comes up, most people are only associating it with its content, or what we feel in any given moment. What most people miss out on in working with their Heart Center is its capacity, otherwise known as our *emotional reactivity*. This differentiation is incredibly important. To work solely on the content of your Heart Center, like me working with my anger and studying the emotion wheel, can be helpful in dealing with issues in your past and ultimately lead to a deeper sense of fulfillment in your life by having access to the whole range of human emotions. But without also working on your emotional reactivity and emotional capacity, your patterns will remain largely intact in times of stress and conflict. Having practices that directly affect both your emotional content and your emotional capacity is crucial for having a fully developed and balanced Heart Center.

Our emotional capacity dictates much of our lives without our even realizing it. We've all been there: you've had a hard day, traffic sucks, and when you get home, the kids are losing their minds. Then, suddenly, despite all those parenting classes and your deeply held belief that all child-conflicts can be handled rationally, you find yourself yelling. Or maybe you've gotten yourself into another fight with your partner about the same thing you always fight about, and then, out of the blue, you're saying you're sorry when you're really not and offering to make dinner and do the dishes just to end the argument, and you end up feeling resentful. While it looks different for each type, our emotional reactivity is the linchpin that holds our type structure in place. When we find ourselves in situations of high stress or threatening conflict, our bodies will react emotionally. This reduces the amount of processing space we have as our heart rates increase, our blood pressure rises, and the stress hormone cortisol is dumped into our bloodstreams. We're in the infamous fight-or-flight mode. From this place, we have little to no ability to make conscious decisions about how to move forward, so we must rely on our patterns. This is where our types take control. If we can work on lessening our emotional reactivity, we will have more space to choose how we would like to respond and will not be forced to rely only on our patterning.

While most people in my workshops and trainings understand that movement practices are the best way to directly affect the body, most of them are stumped when I ask them what practices we can develop to work directly with our Heart Center. I've found most people don't know the answer consciously, but everyone knows it intuitively. The lightbulbs start lighting up as soon as I ask, "What do you tell some-one to do when they're really upset?" "Take a deep breath," everyone in the room responds in unison. Breath work is the most effective practice when dealing with our emotional re-activity because it works directly with our nervous system. Deep breathing slows our heart rates, lowers our blood pres-sure, and lowers cortisol levels in our bodies as well as in-creases our attention to and effectiveness in specific tasks. Breath work directly affects our emotional reactivity and in turn is the key to working on our emotional content and our other centers. Developing the ability to keep our breathing smooth and long throughout difficult situations in our lives and throughout our practices allows us to regulate what's hap-pening in our bodies and through this gives us more space to choose to respond differently to life. As Russ Hudson said so eloquently, "Our patterns depend on shallow breathing."

What does breath work look like? This is another area that modern science is slowly catching on to, but if you want to know the true depth and breadth of what can be accom-plished with breath work, you have to look to the yogic pran-ayama practices. The yogis have developed breathing practices for nearly every kind of situation, but it's important to un-derstand that breath work is never one size fits all. There are breath exercises for calming frazzled nerves, breath practices to help you to feel awake and revitalized, breath practices to aid in digestion, and breath practices to help you feel balanced and focused. The way that you practice each of these will be dependent not only on your type but also on the circumstances of your life in that moment. In my work with clients, I have seen some incredible shifts happen through breath work and have even used it to help people discern their types. I've found in general that the types in the withdrawing triad tend to breathe more into their bellies and less into their chests, causing underbreathing and low energy, while types in the assertive triad tend to breathe more into their chests and less into their bellies, causing a state of ungrounded, high energy that often leads to burnout, and the compliant triad types' breath is short and has a breathless or overcontrolled feel, causing overbreathing and hyperarousal.*

While these are the *tendencies* of each type, each person who leads with that type will have their own experience of the breath. Our breath is incredibly nuanced, and engaging with pranayama practices needs to be overseen by a professional who has been trained in the delicate art of breath work. The breath is an incredibly accessible tool in moments of distress, as it is always with us, and everyone who is alive is always doing it. The only way we will have access to breath as a tool, though, is if we are practicing these techniques regularly when we aren't in distress. A pranayama, or breath work practice, is vital to our personal growth and defusing the time bomb of our emotional reactivity. I highly recommend reaching out to a qualified breath work practitioner to guide your practice, as dealing with issues of your breath on your own can have strong negative effects.

After we have found some space in ourselves by working with our breath and lessening our emotional reactivity,

---

* More on the different triads in the appendix.

we will have more space to develop practices that allow us to work with our emotional content. These practices can be done individually at the beginning of each day or with others in a weekly therapy session or process group. These content practices give us an opportunity to address our type's Emotional Habit as well as the Emotional Filter or Primary Emotion of our dominant center. The Emotional Filter or Primary Emotion for each of the dominant centers is the emotion that each of the triads has the most and easiest access to. In some sense, this is the emotional water each type swims in and because of this can often go unnoticed, unrecognized, and unexpressed. Types in the Body Triad will need to explore their Primary Emotions of anger and resentment, types in the Heart Triad will have to work with their shame and sadness, and types in the Head Triad will need to work on their fear and anxiety. From this initial step, though, each type must address their specific Habit of Emotion, which is the particular set of habits they've developed in the Heart Center.

When working with emotional content, the landscape can seem a little overwhelming. Emotions are unruly and illogical, and most of us have little tolerance for time spent in the Wild West that is our hearts. There are four steps for understanding and working with emotions that help give us a structure to navigate arguably the most unstructured part of ourselves: placing, naming, expressing, and acting.

All of our experience is grounded in our bodies, even our emotions. Taking the time to place our emotions in our physical landscape will make them easier to name but also less overwhelming and all-consuming. When emotions feel overwhelming, we will tend to act out of our patterns in order to calm our emotional seas, and while this works in the short term to alleviate any emotional discomfort, it often has negative long-term repercussions. As you find where an emotion is landing in your body, you can also find where that same emotion is *not* landing in your body, giving you at least a small sense of reprieve from what could initially feel like a deeply overwhelming and challenging experience. Learning to place emotions in the body can be an extensive practice that in and of itself could take years to become proficient in, especially for the head types, who have the majority of their energy displaced upwardly into their Head Center. As you could imagine, the use of physical practices like yoga can be incredibly helpful to prepare you for being able to place an emotion in your body's physical sensations.

After placing the emotion, the next step is naming the emotion. As the saying goes, "What you can't name, you can't change," and while we're not trying to change the emotions we experience, we *are* trying to change the habitual ways we react to them. Naming an emotion can be an entirely internal and personal process; there is no need for anyone else to know exactly what you're experiencing at this point. The naming is for you and is a guide for recognizing emotions and your reactions to them. It's also important to note that there are many emotions for which we don't know the exact right term. As someone who's struggled with emotional vocabulary (remember the emotion wheel?), I've learned that sometimes just giving the sensation a name like "the fluttery one" or "the hot one" can be just as helpful in this process as naming it "infatuation" or "rage." Once the emotion and sensation have a name, the emotion will be easier for you to recognize, which in turn gives you more opportunity to work with and explore both the emotion and how you've responded to it in the past.

After the sensations have been placed and named, it's time to express them—or better phrased, it's time to let ourselves fully experience and express what we feel. Much of Western society tells us that expressing too much emotion makes us irrational or untrustworthy, which leads first to a repression of emotions and then to their explosion. Many of us don't know how to express emotions in ways that are life-giving and lead to deeper connections with those around us, which of course means we need to *practice*. This practice is twofold. We have to be honest about our emotional experience and allow ourselves to embody it fully, and we must also take full responsibility for our emotional states. Honesty means allowing ourselves to be seen in our emotionality. If you're sad, allow yourself to cry; if you're angry, allow yourself to raise your voice and set strong boundaries; if you're scared, allow yourself to tremble. Once we can find a way to be honest with ourselves, with our experiences, and with others, we must realize that our emotions are our responsibility. By taking responsibility for what you feel, you prevent any emotion from becoming an accusation. Moving from "You made me angry!" to "I feel angry" can be a huge leap in our ability to embody and express our emotions in a way that strengthens our relationships instead of tearing them down.

After openly and honestly expressing our emotions, it's important to think about what actions our emotions are asking us to take. What needs are our emotions highlighting for us? Looking to take direct action on behalf of our emotions keeps us from getting stuck in sticky emotional cycles. When we have a headache, we can see that our bodies are possibly asking us for more water or maybe to leave a loud room. When we can see our emotions as signposts or warning lights for our relationships with others and ourselves, just like we can view physical sensations as signs and signals for our physical bodies, we will experience a more meaningful emotional experience as well as stronger and more connected relationships.

After practicing with our physical bodies and our emotional reactivity and experiences, we will have enough space to allow ourselves to practice with our minds.

THE HEAD CENTER
• •

In my sophomore year in high school, I started as a middle blocker on our varsity volleyball team, despite the fact that I was a good three inches shorter than anyone else in our division playing that position. I was certainly the underdog, and I loved the challenge of it. I had a great vertical leap and almost perfect timing. I was determined to play Division I volleyball in college and had no problem putting in the work to make it happen. I was in the gym training, conditioning, and lifting three times a day. Then one day in practice, I came down wrong on my right leg and blew out my knee. I didn't want to let that stop me, though. After surgery and three months of rehab, I was back on the court. But something was different. I couldn't move as quickly, I certainly couldn't jump as high, and my body just didn't work the way I wanted it to. My mind could see the plays I needed to make, but my body couldn't make them happen. I was devastated.

My knee injury marked the end of my athletic career, but as I look back, I realize it wasn't my knee that was the problem—it was my head. I was still seeing the court and thinking through plays as if nothing had happened to my body. My attention was focused on the wrong things, and the way I was thinking didn't work for how my body could move now. My mind was stuck in the old patterns of seeing and thinking, and I didn't know how to shift it. We've all run into situations in our lives where the ways we used to see and think no longer work for us, and these times are often extremely challenging for us. This is because working with our minds (the most subtle of the three centers) may be the most difficult aspect of working on ourselves.

As we move toward higher and higher energies, and more and more subtle sensations in the Head Center, it is incredibly important to make clear—to the best of our ability—what we're talking about. There are two main components to our Head Center: attention and thoughts. These two functions of the Head Center correlate to our center's capacity and content, respectively. Similarly to how we worked with the Heart Center, it is almost always easiest to address our Head Center's capacity before addressing its content.

Our attention is quite literally our ability to see—not just with our physical eyes, but to see and to experience all of what life is bringing to us physically, emotionally, mentally, and even spiritually. We have an external attention that we use to be aware of cars on the road or find our beloved in a crowd of people, but humans also have an *internal* attention. Because of this higher level of attention, we are able to self-reflect. We are capable of knowing what we are doing as we do it. We are (or at least we have the capacity to be) self-aware. Sadly, for most of us, our attention becomes something of an underdeveloped muscle. It will begin to function habitually, creating each type's Habit of Attention. Working with our Habit of Attention is the first step in working with the energies of the Head Center. Some people see this as trying to directly shift their type's Habit of Attention, be it correcting errors, fighting against injustice, or seeing what's missing. In reality, though, it is more like a workout program for the muscle of our attention.

So what does training your attention look like? Simply put: meditation. Meditation is the most effective tool we have for directly addressing and strengthening our attention, but what, exactly, is meditation? And why is everyone so bad at it? The answer to the latter is because very few people actually know the answer to the former. As a yoga therapist, I hear it almost every day: "I'm bad at meditation" or "Oh, I can't meditate." Our culture by and large has been sold the idea that meditation is reserved for the calmest and most serene among us—or even worse, only neurotypical people. So many of us have fallen for the idea that meditation is "emptying your mind" or "having no thoughts." While these phrases get thrown around in the meditation world, they are hardly meant to be a definition of what meditation is and are often more misleading and confusing than helpful. According to prominent yoga therapist and meditation teacher Chase Bossart, meditation is simply this: directed attention. When we look at meditation not as an annihilation of our thoughts but as directing our attention, suddenly meditation as a practice feels very much within reach.

We direct our attention every day to tasks, to conversations, to our habituated thought patterns. Like I mentioned in the last chapter, though, our attention tends to go where it will, and if we aren't conscious of it, it will continue to direct itself toward the same things over and over. Meditation is simply the task of consciously choosing what we pay attention to.

Because meditation's definition is so simple, it opens up the doors to many different styles of meditation. Meditation could be sitting and focusing on your breath, or it could be envisioning a large mountain. It could be taking your attention throughout your body, or it could be chanting a mantra. The meditation can be guided by a teacher or even an app, or it could be fully self-directed. What all of these practices have in common is that they require us to keep our attention focused and be aware of what we're focusing on. This awareness and concentration are what help us refine our Head Center. The longer we are able to direct our attention on things of our choosing, the less likely we will be to fall into our unconscious Habit of Attention; the more we can watch our patterned and habitual thoughts instead of getting wrapped up in them, the more we'll be able to keep ourselves from running in circles around the issues of our lives. These are the basics of our capacity practices for our Head Center.

As always, though, capacity is only half the battle. Just like the other centers, the *content* of our Head Center must be addressed. Working with our thoughts can be tricky, but the following steps can be a helpful guide in working with our habitual thought patterns.

If we want to shift our thinking, we must begin by actually knowing what we're thinking in the first place. This requires *listening*. As we learn to listen to our thoughts instead of just reacting to them or being wrapped up in them, we'll gain a greater understanding of what's happening for us internally. It's important to remember that, just like all other types of true self-observation, this listening has to be nonjudgmental, meaning we can't assign positive or negative feelings to our thoughts. Our job at this point is just to listen.

Once we've really listened to our thoughts, we can more easily recognize how our thoughts are playing into our type's patterns. Someone who leads with type 4 may hear a lot of thoughts romanticizing the past, while someone who leads with type 7 may be continually planning out their next great adventure. Just because our thoughts clearly align with our type doesn't mean that they are either good or bad; they're simply part of our pattern. As we see our thoughts in the context of our type, it becomes easier to see what might be triggering or leading to these repetitive thoughts. For example, I know that when I catch myself in a daydream about doing something superheroesque, I'm usually feeling helpless or vulnerable around something. My thoughts use the daydream to help me reassert my sense of control and capability.

Once you can listen to your thoughts and place them in the context of your type, then it's time to question them. Are they helpful? Are they true? Are they based in reality? Is there another way to look at things? These questions can be incredibly hard to ask of ourselves and often even harder to answer. All of our thoughts are interconnected with our emotions, so often our habitual thought patterns are tied to some pretty deep emotions, which don't like to be challenged. Asking and honestly answering these questions, though, gives us the space to move into more productive thinking and be more consciously critical of the thoughts that constantly pop in and out of our minds.

If simply questioning the thought patterns isn't enough to inspire change, using affirmations will often get you the rest of the way. Putting affirmations to work is the practice of intentionally thinking new thoughts. This actually helps us build new neural pathways in the brain, and the more we use them, the more efficient we become at using them and the easier we'll be able to think those more helpful thoughts when we need them. I used this practice extensively while I was building my business. I noticed how easy it was for me to shift into a state of panic anytime someone canceled a session, and that panic made it nearly impossible for me to effectively handle the rest of my work. After a few of these panic sessions, I started using the affirmation "I plant seeds of calm abundance," and soon this was enough to shift my thinking and help me steer clear of a lot of the unnecessary emotional turmoil of entrepreneurship.

PUTTING IT ALL TOGETHER

When we set out to develop a practice, we should be intentional in including specific practices for all three of our centers. As we've seen, the Head Center is by far the most subtle of the three. This makes it much more difficult to work with but also that much more powerful and rewarding when we can actually make it happen. This subtlety is why we begin our practice with the body, then move to the Heart Center, and then move to the Head Center. As we move from the more gross, we gain more access to the aspects of ourselves and our centers that are more subtle. When most people talk about personal or spiritual development, they're talking about developing their minds or their hearts, while working on the body is seen as vain or superficial. The reality, though, is that working with the body, when done correctly, acts as a backdoor access to our hearts and our minds. Having practices that directly affect how our bodies function will also indirectly affect our other two centers and make it easier for us to develop them as well. As we work with the body, we'll have more access to how our emotions show up in our physical sensations, which makes them easier to work with. As we do more work with our bodies and our hearts, we'll have more space and energy to address the habitual thought patterns that unconsciously drive us. As we develop practices that address all of who we are, we open ourselves up more fully to the possibility of what we could be.

CHAPTER 3

PRACTICE BEST PRACTICES

When I was first training to be a yoga therapist, and then an Enneagram teacher, I had some pretty big ideas about what my job would look like on the other side of all this learning and training. I would most certainly be sought out to enlighten people to the challenges their types were causing them and would know exactly what practices would bring them back into balance. We could plumb the depths of the Yoga Sutras and be guided by the Enneagram into new heights of personal understanding. People would come to me with their problems and I would share the wisdom of the Enneagram and the practical tools of yoga, and then people would leave and enjoy their newfound peace, love, and happiness. Simple as that. It was a very dreamy dream indeed.

Clearly my imagination had gotten the best of me. The reality is that the vast majority of my job as both a yoga therapist and an Enneagram coach actually bears little resemblance to that fantasy. Sure, I listen to people and help them see their issues in the context of their type, and I work with them to build practices to help them shift their perception around these issues, but I don't do that nearly as much as I once expected I would. What I do most is simply this: coach behavior change. It's a relatively easy thing to develop a practice either for yourself or for someone else. What is difficult about my job is helping people actually *do* their practice. It is incredibly challenging to move out of our patterns and routines, whether they're the ways our types function or even the way we drive to work each day. Changing our patterns requires a lot of energy and sends ripples of change out into every aspect of our lives and even into the lives of those around us. It's daunting to create new habits, and even when we know what to do, it can be hard to know *how* to do it. In this chapter, my goal is to bring you as much tangible advice as I can about how to develop your own daily practice that helps you gain more freedom from your personality patterns and moves you into the deep and meaningful life you are meant to live. I'm also going to showcase a few case studies of how my clients have developed their practices and the benefit it's had on their lives.

Let's clear the air about what to expect from our practices right of out of the gate. If our expectations are too high—or even just off-base—when we start, we'll easily get discouraged and give up. I want to bust a few myths about personal and spiritual practices to give you the best chance of success. We seem to have some pretty lofty expectations about our spiritual and personal practices: that they will keep us from experiencing hard things, or that they make us good people, or that they're like a drug—something we can take to make ourselves instantly feel better. When these expectations surround our practice, we will be trying to achieve something that our practices aren't designed for and judge ourselves and our practices accordingly. These judgments and perceived failures end up doing more damage than not having a practice at all. So if we're going to embark on this journey, it's best to understand where our practices are actually taking us.

We practice developing presence and awareness of what we're experiencing in the moment. From this presence, awareness, and capacity to experience what life brings to us, we will be able to choose how to respond in ways that will bring us more depth of connection with those around us and a more meaningful and fulfilling life. But our practice doesn't do this on its own. Sitting down to meditate for twenty minutes twice a day won't magically turn you into the Dalai Lama. What it will do is create more space for you to choose what you'd like to do instead of being run by your patterns. To quote Victor Frankl, "Between stimulus and response there is a space," and the bigger that space, the easier it will be for you to make decisions that your type would find foreign. But you still have to make that decision; your practice won't do it for you. In sports, practice makes you a better player, but you still have to show up and play the game. Our practices should never be an escape from life but should instead equip us to meet all of life with more openness.

I work with people every day who come in and tell me that they had another anxiety attack, or that they're still feeling depressed, or that the problem they've been working on is *still a problem*, and they feel like they're failing at their practice or that it's the wrong one. So many people assume that if "bad" things are happening to them, their practice must not be working. I've seen this so many times with my clients and experienced it more times than I'd like to admit in my own life that I came up with this helpful reminder: "Practice does not prevent; practice prepares." If you struggle with anxiety, you will still struggle with anxiety even if you're doing a personal practice. If you are depressed, there is a good chance that you will still deal with depressive episodes even if you're doing a daily personal practice. Now, of course our circumstances may shift as we do our practices, but where the real change occurs is in our ability to hold these circumstances and respond to them in the best way possible. You may still experience anxiety attacks, but you will be able to respond to them differently. Our practices don't prevent these uncomfortable things from happening. Our practices prepare us for these uncomfortable things. Would it make sense that practicing your favorite instrument would make the recital disappear? Would you do your drills and fundamentals in baseball if it made the possibility of playing in the World Series nonexistent? Of course not!

Practice really is the best word for what we're doing. We are practicing for how we want to show up in the world when life is less than ideal. Our practices are not a magic wand that we can wave to turn our lives into fairy tales. Our practices do, however, create a very magical change inside of us, giving us the room to fully hold and fully heal what our less-than-fairytale lives send our way.

Many people are quickly turned off by the idea of a personal practice, not because they don't want to be making these changes in their lives but because of the attitude so many practicing people have. It can be easy to both assume and then begin to act as if doing a practice makes you a better person than everyone else. We've all met that person who just started meditating two weeks ago and can't stop talking about it, we all know someone who's been to therapy twice and suddenly has the solutions to all our problems, and we probably even know quite a few Enneagram enthusiasts who are certain they know your type better than you do. I jokingly call this the Spiritual Superiority Complex, and it is surprisingly insidious. It seems obvious in people who walk around with their noses in the air after they've completed their practices, but it can also show up in much more subtle ways. I've noticed, for example, that I have a certain piece of my self-esteem wrapped up in my practice. Whenever I let my practice go for a time, I feel a heavy sense of shame for having let it lapse. The truth is, I have a hard time believing I'm a good person if I'm not keeping my practice, which means that somewhere in the dark reaches of my subconscious mind, I believe that keeping my practice makes me a better person. This is a troublesome belief because it makes missing my practice for a couple of days a moral failing instead of a scheduling issue or a matter of needing more sleep. This perceived moral failing then makes it more difficult to begin again, as I've fallen into a shame spiral and my self-esteem has taken a hit. Suddenly, getting back to my practice has the weight of my personal value stacked upon it, when in reality, my practice is simply something that creates space for me. Of course, I would like to do it every day, but missing a day doesn't make me a bad person, and my day isn't totally ruined simply because I didn't start it by moving and breathing in an intentional way.

Believing that our practices are something like a magic bullet can make them difficult to stick with. So many teachers tout the benefits of practice and make them out to be some sort of cure-all that will transform our lives overnight. Our culture is desperate for quick fixes, and we're always looking for the easy button. The thing about practice is it's less like a magic pill and more like a lifestyle. It's a series of small changes that create momentum over time. While a great yoga class or a powerful meditation can directly and immediately affect your system in a way that may make you think, feel, and move differently for a short time, the real lasting effects of our practices build up over time. As we say in the yoga community, the real change doesn't happen on the mat, it happens when you step off it. When we look at our practices more like a lifestyle and less like a drug, we can be more patient with the way things shift in us. If we expect our practice to always drastically alter our consciousness every time we step on the mat, we're going to be deeply disappointed.

TIPS FOR BUILDING YOUR PRACTICE
• •

Once we've cleared our consciousness of these unconscious beliefs, it's time to start crafting our own practices. Now, it's easy to get lost in all the ins and outs of building your own practice, but it doesn't have to be so complicated. I like to tell my clients, "The best practice is the one you do." They don't have to be fancy or impressive; just taking five minutes to breathe deeply before you head into a stressful workday can drastically improve your life. Clients come to me expecting some hour-long practice that involves cardio and standing on their head, but more often than not we start with a very small breathing practice. We move slowly in order to make the changes real and lasting. From my years of working with clients, I've compiled what I believe to be the best tips and pointers for building your own practice.

Start Where You Are

When starting our personal practices, it's important to remember we're starting from scratch—or maybe more accurately, we're starting with all of our negative and unhelpful patterns very much intact. This means that we can't expect ourselves to suddenly have some superhuman ability to change ourselves overnight. As an 8, I need to practice being gentle and working with subtlety, but my introduction to personal practice was actually quite intense and forceful. I started practicing Baptiste-style power yoga, which is basically designed to push your body to the limits. My type *loved* it. I liked pushing myself and enjoyed feeling strong because of it. Of course, that kind of intense physical activity was great for a time, but the intensity soon became problematic, just like our patterns. Because I had developed a daily practice, though, I wasn't interested in giving it up altogether but changing it to something more appropriate instead. Before I began my yoga practice, I hated the slow and gentle types of yoga, but after indulging in my patterns a little bit, the slower approach became more appealing. Sometimes we have to give our type a little of what it wants in order to create something that helps it relax its grip on us. In other words, whatever gets you to your practice to begin with is good and valuable. We need to honor these starting points while also realizing we might not stay there forever.

Use What You Have

One of the biggest pitfalls I see people encounter in developing their own practice is their desire for more stuff. Our culture is convinced that in order to do things correctly, we have to have all the latest gear—for example, thinking that you can't start your practice until you have that new yoga mat or the best app for timing your breathing or meditation. I fall victim to this quite frequently, but one of the reasons I love my personal practice is that I don't actually *need* any of that stuff. You don't need anything special to do a practice. You already have everything you need. No yoga mat? No problem. Don't have one of those fancy meditation stools? Who cares! All you need for your practice is you.

Do What You Can

Your practice should always be something within your reach. Yes, a practice on occasion may push you up to your edge, but it should never push you past that edge. Change through our practices happens gradually over time, and you should never ask yourself or your system to practice something that is clearly outside of your current abilities. A 6 client of mine once told me they couldn't meditate. Of course, I whole-heartedly disagreed with them, but I asked them why. They said there was no way they could sit still and be quiet for a whole twenty minutes, since their mind was just running in too many different directions. I asked them if they could sit still and quiet for two minutes, to which they replied, "Well, sure." So, we started their meditation practice there. Slowly over time it grew, and now they're sitting still and quiet for twenty minutes twice a day! Had they tried to force them-selves to sit for the full twenty minutes at the start, they would have quickly become discouraged and given up, but starting where they did gave them the opportunity to move to where they wanted to go.

Move, Breathe, Meditate

There is a reason that I ordered our centers the way I did in the last chapter. When building a practice, it's best to start with the most accessible center and then move to the least. I believe that, regardless of your type, starting with the body is the best way to move through all three centers in a single practice. Starting with the body means we're starting with the most obvious part of ourselves, allowing us to move into our breath, which directly affects our Heart Center. After we have focused both our Body and Heart Centers, we will have more ability to focus our minds because we've already directed or burned off our excess physical and emotional energy. In some sense, working this way "clears a path" to the more subtle energies of the mind. Working first with the body and then with the emotional center is something of a handhold at the crux of working with our Head Center.

Frequency over Duration

Diving into an hour-long practice might completely change your life, but if you can only do that hour once a week, it's going to have less impact on you and your system than practicing for only ten minutes six days a week. This is be-cause our practices become a touchstone for us to return to throughout our days, in times of stress or turmoil. If the last time we got to experience our practice was a week ago, it will be a hazy memory to try to cling to, even if it was deeply impactful at the time. Conversely, even if our practice didn't feel particularly affecting, but the last time we engaged with it was only a few hours ago, the experience will be easier to access when we're in need.

Consistency is key. Having a set time of day for our practice helps our bodies, hearts, and minds find and stay in a rhythm. Our systems begin to rely on our practices happening at a certain time and flourish because of it. It may not always be possible, but the more consistent you are with the time of day of your practice, the easier it will be to integrate its benefits into your life. In addition to time of day, where you do your practice matters. Having a small space dedicated to your practice, or at least a place you can come back to each day, makes it easier to do the practice each day. This space also creates a sense of safety that allows you to move deeper into your practice. The space itself plays a part in your practice by becoming its container.

Those are the veritable "do's" of having a practice, and you can bet that if there are "do's," there are going to be some "don'ts." I like to think of these more like warning signs than things to avoid because, honestly, they are unavoidable. These things will happen from time to time, and it's important to be aware of them and be aware of how to correct them.

THINGS TO WATCH OUT FOR

Reinforcing Your Patterns

It is so crucial to find a practice that works for you that you enjoy but that *also* challenges the patterns of your type. Our types are sneaky and will find their way into everything we do, *especially* our personal or spiritual practices. I like to tell the story of how I first developed a spiritual practice: I had never done a power yoga class before, but after just one, I was hooked. It clearly resonated with my type-8 structure, which as I mentioned earlier isn't necessarily a bad thing, but it wasn't actually inviting me into something different from my patterns. It can be helpful to ask yourself what you like about your practices and how your practices align with your type. These things aren't inherently bad, but you will want to pay attention to them as you continue on your path to avoid reinforcing the patterns you're hoping to loosen in your life. Type 8s, like I mentioned, will often find practices that feed a sense of intensity, 6s may seek out something where they are being led instead of leading themselves, 4s may reach for the most obscure or interesting practice. These are all generalizations on some pretty basic type stereotypes, but they help illustrate what to watch out for.

Your Practices Changing Too Much
In our fast-paced world, we want to find the perfect practice, and we want to find it now. This often means that people will change their practice far too frequently. If there's something just slightly off about it, or we don't feel a dramatic shift in our consciousness right away, we will tend to abandon it in hopes of finding that exact perfect practice somewhere else. The trouble is that this tendency is often only reinforcing our patterns. It is important to give our practices time and space to do their work. Our patterns are subtle, and the practices we use to work with them are also subtle. We may not feel the effects of our hard work for some time, but that doesn't mean it isn't working or it's not the right practice. Some of the more hardcore yoga teachers have said that a practice must be done every day for forty days before it's clear if it needs to be changed. This may seem extreme, but it's important to

give your practices a fair shake, and I often suggest to clients that they do their practice for at least a month before making any major adjustments (as long as it's not causing any physical pain or dramatically making their symptoms worse).

Your Practices Staying the Same Too Long

Just as jumping around from practice to practice will keep us from experiencing the full benefits of them, staying in a practice too long keeps us from growing and developing further. We develop our practice in order to work through specific issues we're facing, and if our practice is effective, those issues will become less and less troublesome for us, but over time we'll likely have a whole new slew of issues to work with. When this happens, it's time for our practice to shift and change, just like we've shifted and changed. The Enneagram does such a wonderful job of showing us how detailed and dynamic we are, and our practices should be the same. I practiced Centering Prayer for the better part of a decade. It was absolutely revolutionary in my life and my relationship with the divine. It was the perfect practice that met me at the perfect time. As I grew and developed, though, it was no longer serving me in the way it once had. My teacher recommended I try a different meditation for a while, and I was shocked at how quickly it took effect. We often develop a sincere affinity for our practices, especially if we've done them for a long period of time. This can make changing things up difficult. I was very resistant when my teacher first suggested trying something new, but I can see now that these new practices have truly furthered the work that Centering Prayer started within me.

Falling Asleep to Your Practice

We often experience a certain excitement as we embark on this journey of inner work. This excitement is incredibly helpful for keeping ourselves present as we do our practices. However, this energy and excitement fades as our practices become more routine and mundane. If our ability to stay focused and present in our practice fades with the initial excitement, we won't experience the fullness our practices have to offer us. Sure, movement is movement, and moving will make your body feel better, but without our presence and Conscious Attention, we will miss out on the opportunity to build a more meaningful relationship with our bodies. Whatever practice you take up, it will have its intrinsic value, whether it's movement, breathing, meditation, walking, and so on, but when we engage in any of these practices with the fullness of our Conscious Attention, we're invited into something more transformative than just the simple actions we're performing. Falling asleep to our practices (doing them without Conscious Attention) happens from time to time for everyone. It may mean you need to change locations or maybe that it's time to switch up your practices. Whatever the cause, if the lack of energy and attention in our practices continues, we will be at risk of not only not getting the most out of our practices but letting our practices fall away completely.

HOW TO DO THE DOS AND AVOID THE DON'TS
. . . .

This is probably that part of the book where you're expecting me to write out a personal practice for each type to help them transform themselves. But I'm not going to do that. Our personal practices are much too sacred, and we as people are far too complex to simply list out what each type should be doing with their body, breath, and attention. Two different people of the same type could be almost infinitely different, and thus their practices would need to reflect those differences. So even though it's what people ask for most, I can't in good conscience give blanket type-based practices. There are, however, some things that each type can keep in mind and be aware of as they go about their practices. Think of these as helpful bumpers and guideposts along the path.

Type 9: With your tendency to forget yourself and give in to the inertia of situations, it's important to continually check in with yourself about your practice. Are you in it? Are you really experiencing it? Or are you going through the motions? It is also extremely important to remember that in order to grow, we have to make ourselves uncomfortable. This doesn't simply mean giving up what you want in order to be more "holy" or "righteous." For you, dear 9, this will likely mean stepping into the deep discomfort of standing on your own and standing up for what you know to be right.

Type 8: No one can deny your strength and power, dear 8, so maybe you don't always have to try to prove it to yourself and everyone else. Your intensity pushes you forward, often into things that are unhelpful, and at the very least has you putting more effort into things than is necessary. Embracing subtlety and gentleness is difficult work for you because it asks you to become aware of how the world is really impacting you, but this is your work. And this is slow work. No amount of pushing or leaning forward in your chair will get you there any faster. Instead, try sitting back and relaxing into all your practices. Can you stop making things harder than they need to be?

Type 7: Your desire to experience everything you can often leaves you floating on the surface of life, dear 7. If your practices have you jumping around too much, or they change too often, there's a good chance your type has taken charge again. Practices that require you to slow down, stay focused, and confront your discomfort will take you the farthest on this journey. They can even open up in you a new experience, one of constancy and stability. These are things to be savored and enjoyed!

Type 6: There will be pros and cons to every practice you could ever possibly participate in, but remember that any practice is better than none. Your mind is overworked, so don't let choosing a practice cause any more stress. Using your body and your breath to lower the volume on your experience will help make room for you to relax. And remember, cultivating a sense of safety in your body takes time; don't write off the process if it doesn't come naturally right off the bat, dear 6.

Type 5: Dear 5, you are considered the Enneagram's most natural contemplative, but contemplation is nothing without action. Pay attention to your tendency to live in your ivory tower. Are your practices keeping you and your wisdom under lock and key? Can you cultivate practices that bring you out into the world? While you've gained knowledge through your intellectual capacities, your body holds a wisdom that knows no limits. Practices that focus solely on the mind and neglect the body won't take you anywhere you haven't already been, so be sure to get up and move.

Type 4: As much as it may seem boring and mundane, dear 4, routine is going to be your best friend in this process. The more you can create a sense of regularity in your daily life, the more of your energy you can spend on the things that are really important to you. Your practice should help you establish this routine, regardless of how you feel about it from day to day. Please keep in mind that if you're judging your practice solely on what it elicits in you emotionally, your type will continue to toss you back and forth like a small raft on a choppy sea.

Type 3: It's all the rage right now to share about your practices online, dear 3, and while that may help with a sense of accountability, beware of your tendency to perform. Any time your practice has an audience, there will be the temptation for you to perform your practice instead of experience it. Solo practices are recommended. Ask yourself: Who are you doing your practice for? If the answer is anyone but you, it may be time to check in and adjust. Remember, there is no way to succeed or fail at your practice. It just is.

Type 2: Remember, dear 2, that you keep your practice because *you need it*, not because anyone else needs you to show up differently in your life. When you notice yourself wrapping your motivation up in how well you can meet other people's needs, you're only practicing feeling ashamed. Your practice is just for you because you deserve to show up for yourself, even if it gets in the way of showing up for other people. Practices that help you set and keep boundaries and limits will make the process smoother.

Type 1: Dear 1, there is no right way to have a practice. Please read that again because it's the truth. When you feel the desire to perfect your practices or the need to do them "just so," it may be time to stop and take a deep breath. There is a power much larger than the particularities of your practice at play when you can just allow yourself to show up as you are and be OK with that. Practices that help you actively relax the tension in your body can spur you on in the mental and emotional journey of self-acceptance. Consider making a practice out of giving yourself a break, not because you've already achieved so much or because you're so far ahead of the rest of us, but simply because you're human.

All these do's and don'ts might feel overwhelming, especially when you're already starting something that is intrinsically difficult. But don't worry—you can take things one step at a time. Your practice doesn't have to be perfect when you first start it. You may have false starts and detours, and that's all part of the process. The most important thing to remember is that the best practice is the one you do and, I might add, *keep doing.* For as trite as it may sound, sometimes you just have to stick with it, and while "just sticking with it" brings its own difficulties, there is one thing you can do to make all of this easier: get a mentor.

Like most endeavors in life, trying to build a practice all on your own will make the process much more difficult, much less enjoyable, and much less rewarding. Working with someone who is qualified to help you develop your personal or spiritual practices will ensure that you build a strong and transformative practice that works for *you.* Having someone who has been where you are and has moved beyond it as a guide is the best way to ensure that you are working at something that will work for you and keep you from slipping into all of those pesky "don'ts." You may have been working on your personal practice for many years or may just be starting out, but wherever you find yourself on this journey, there is someone out there who can enrich your experience if you're willing to be in right relationship with them. In the next section of this book, we'll discuss how having a qualified mentor or teacher can help you not only with your practice but with the whole of your spiritual or personal growth journey.

LEG II

LINEAGE

CHAPTER 4
LEARNING FROM THE FLOW

I started rock climbing in early 2019. At first it was just a way to be active—I needed a new way of moving to help manage some mental health issues that had been becoming increasingly severe over the months prior. After maybe the third or fourth session, though, it was clear that I was developing a serious passion for the sport. I met with a small group of friends weekly to climb together, and soon I was climbing nearly every day on my own. I got myself a job teaching yoga at one of our local climbing gyms so I could afford to have memberships at that gym and the one across town. I was deeply passionate about climbing. I felt like I came alive on the wall, and my abilities progressed quickly. I spent my free time watching YouTube videos about all the best gear and what techniques to practice. A few months later, though, I hit the dreaded "grade plateau." Of course, I knew all about the "grade plateaus," where you can't seem to move up to the next level of difficulty in your climbing, because they're a common topic of videos, blogs, and

Instagram posts. It seems everyone wants to know how to move past these plateaus. I dove into the advice, and honestly, not much worked—I just felt stuck.

That's when the words of my yoga teacher, Chase Bossart, rang in my head: "Get a mentor." It was probably the biggest joke of our yoga therapy class, and we always said it as if it were in all caps. Chase would repeat it upward of ten times every class as he shared with us about the Bhagavad Gita or the Panca Maya Model. It was his go-to catchphrase, and I'm sure he could even work it into a lesson about South American tree frogs. I had already experienced how helpful a mentor could be in other areas of my life—with my business, my relationship, and my spiritual journey—so it seemed like a no-brainer that mentorship would also work with climbing. I reached out to one of the climbers who taught private lessons at my local gym and started working with him for a couple of months. Even just after our first session, I saw a dramatic improvement in how I was moving on the wall, and as we continued to work together, I was suddenly able to integrate and apply things that I had struggled with for months. I was getting stronger and more skilled on the wall. I was also climbing faster than when I first started, which felt exhilarating. When I eventually hit another plateau, my coach was supportive and encouraging and was able to adjust what we focused on to address my personal struggles. My coach shared from his personal experience, having gone through similar situations in his climbing journey, and helped me avoid some of the more common pitfalls that arise when dealing with "grade plateaus."

Finding a coach was the best thing I had ever done in my climbing journey, and, honestly, it's also the best thing I've ever done in my personal life and for my relationship and parenting. But I have to come clean and admit that the first time I heard Chase lecture our class on the importance of having a personal mentor and teacher, I sat back with arms crossed and thought to myself, "Nah, I've got it." The whole idea just seemed off. Paying someone money to have them tell me how to live my life and do my job? No, thank you. I mean, isn't that how awful scandals happen? Some self-appointed self-help guru gains a whole bunch of followers, and then said guru does a whole bunch of bad things to said followers? I had no intention of being brainwashed or joining a cult, so clearly, I didn't need a "teacher."

Since that day, I pulled a total 180 and now have a yoga therapist and mentor (who I will henceforth lovingly refer to as "my teacher") whose influence on my life has become absolutely invaluable to me. Have I been brainwashed by a charismatic leader and surrendered all personal autonomy? Absolutely not. Through the process of first realizing I need a teacher and then building that relationship, I learned a lot about myself, and I'm a better person for it. I have a deep and intimate understanding of why so many people are averse to the idea of having a personal teacher or mentor because I was one of those people. Western culture, especially in America, is highly individualistic and tends to make each of us believe that we must "go it alone," that it's "you against the world." We do the majority of our learning in classroom settings, where the information is thrown up on the board, and it's our job to absorb as much as we can. Rarely do we develop long-lasting and meaningful relationships with teachers, which isn't surprising given the cultural narrative we have around the teacher/student relationship. Whether it's Freud teaching Jung, Jesus teaching Judas, or Obi-Wan teaching Anakin, everything is all fine and good until there's some sort of conflict or disagreement, and suddenly the fate of the galaxy hangs in the balance. Even the Enneagram itself has a sordid history of teacher/student relationships gone wrong.* So how can I sit here and write about the need for a personal teacher? Do we really need all that drama in the information age? Can't we just google it?

I love using the example of my climbing journey because the results were so tangible. I had devoured all the internet resources available on how to move through plateaus and what gear was the best for what stage and style of climbing I found myself in, and all of that helped me progress a little bit. But I wasn't able to move past my plateau until I found a teacher. Developing a personal relationship with a teacher or mentor in our personal and spiritual work with the Enneagram is absolutely vital. Throughout this section of the book, we'll explore what a teacher gives us that we can't get from other nonhuman information sources, what makes a good teacher and a good student, and how being aware of where our information comes from will change what we are able to do with it.

WHAT TEACHERS GIVE US
• •

It's easy to believe that the era of needing to seek out a teacher or some sort of ascended master to teach us the things we need to know is long past. We live in the information age!

---

* See the "History" section of the appendix.

I have all the world's knowledge sitting in my back pocket right now; why on earth would I need a teacher?! The truth is that information only gets us so far, and often, information on its own doesn't point us in the right direction. Of course, for some things you want to learn, like changing a headlight in your car, looking up an instructional video on YouTube may serve you best. But if you were interested in becoming a mechanic, you'd do well to find yourself an experienced mechanic to apprentice under. This is why it's so important to find an experienced and qualified Enneagram teacher to learn from: we aren't just trying to change the occasional headlight; we're trying to understand how the whole car works.

A qualified and experienced teacher, whether they're teaching us the Enneagram or how to change our oil, offers us three main things that we can't get from simply reading a book or watching a video. These three things, *perspective*, *being*, and *lineage*, are fundamental on our spiritual journey. We won't get far without them, and we can't get them without a teacher.

PERSPECTIVE

Before I had a climbing coach, I would try to climb with other people as much as possible. I loved having someone on the ground who could tell me what I was doing while I was on the wall. It was so incredibly helpful in my climbing journey, but what I noticed about my friend's feedback is that it often had more to do with how *they* would do the climb and a lot less about how *I* could do the climb. Now, this isn't to say their advice wasn't helpful—often it was! But there was something distinctly different in the way my coach gave suggestions and advice about my climbing; it was clear he was talking about *my climb*, and *my body*, not his. Many people in our lives can offer us perspective, but a qualified and experienced teacher offers us something more: a clear perspective. For someone to have a clear perspective, they have to work to understand how they see the world *and* how the other person sees the world.

Now, it's impossible to be completely objective in any situation. Pure objectivity is a myth—it simply doesn't exist in this world. Every person has their own personal slant on things, and those slants make a person's guidance incredibly helpful at times and incredibly harmful at others (more on this later on in the chapter). A qualified teacher, though, has been trained not to erase or try to see past their own perspective but to see it more clearly and, from there, be able to work with it more effectively. To return to the car analogy, if I was trying to change the oil in my Mitsubishi Outlander, but I was asking a mechanic who only worked on Fords, I would inevitably run into some issues. Now, if this mechanic thought they knew all cars instead of realizing they only worked on Fords, they would try to give me advice that wouldn't fit for my car. If, instead, the mechanic was a good teacher and acknowledged their own perspective and bias, they would likely take a closer look at my vehicle and the differences therein. Then they could give me more helpful advice about where to find specific engine parts or possibly give me the name of a mechanic who works solely on Mitsubishis. When a teacher understands their own perspective and their many inherent biases, they can then begin to see and eventually understand someone more clearly, sometimes even more clearly than the person themselves. This kind of perspective is absolutely critical for our journeys with the Enneagram.

The kind of perspective I get from my teacher and give to my own clients can be broken down into two styles: external and internal. When it comes to explaining the value of external perspective, I love the Buddhist parable from the ancient Indian subcontinent about the five blind people who come across an elephant. One person touches just the tail and thinks it's a rope, one person touches the leg and thinks it's a tree, one person touches the trunk and thinks it's a big snake, one person touches the elephant's side and believes it to be a wall, and one person touches the tusk and thinks it's a spear. None of these people who are up close and personal with this elephant have any idea what they're actually encountering, and that is nearly always the case when we face our own personal challenges, especially in Enneagram work. Having a teacher who can see things a few steps removed can help us put all those pieces together and see the real elephant we're dealing with. This is external perspective: someone standing far enough away from our situation to see it clearly.

A few months into writing this book, my mental health took a pretty big dip. I figured it was just exhaustion, but taking a few days off to really focus on self-care wasn't doing the trick, and it felt like things just got worse. When I brought all of this up to my teacher, she was able to draw my attention out of the immediate struggle and help me see the bigger picture of several years lived at full tilt with a lot of life events that I hadn't yet taken the time to process or emotionally digest. So while taking a few baths and focusing on my self-care routines was helpful in the short term, it wasn't until I started addressing the real elephant in the room that my mental and emotional health started to shift and change for the better.

Many people in our lives can offer us external perspective—friends, family, sometimes even strangers on the street—but internal perspective is more nuanced. Take my climbing buddies as an example: I had a lot of people offering suggestions and advice, but a real coach's perspective ended up being more helpful in the long run because he was far enough along in his own journey that he had perspective on his own early struggles and how to move through them. This made it easier for him to see what I was doing more clearly, without projecting his own stuff onto what I was going through. This kind of perspective isn't just from someone at a distance; it's from someone who has been through something similar and has already worked through it and mentally and emotionally digested it. Just as we each get more perspective on our struggles years after they've ended, our teachers and mentors have too. While we may be in the thick of some nasty challenge, if we've picked a qualified and experienced teacher, they're already on the other side of this kind of quagmire and can offer the most helpful suggestions for moving through it with grace and ease.

Clear internal and external perspective is absolutely vital to our journey with the Enneagram. I have had not only the pleasure of working with a teacher who has offered me this kind of perspective but also the deep honor of offering it to my own students and clients. The Enneagram is already a wonderful tool for helping people gain more perspective. It's an incredible map for our journey, but without a teacher to reflect to us where we are and what we're going through, we'll be left driving in circles. My clients and I often laugh about how simple things are once we get the right perspective. It's downright hilarious how often we can't see what's right in front of our faces! A 6 client of mine went on and on about their struggles with their close friends—how they didn't speak up and ask for what they needed but always showed up for their friends even if the favor was never returned. To them, all of this felt like their world was caving in, and they couldn't hold themself up under the weight of it all. Once I gently suggested that maybe this had something to do with their 6ness and their need to be loyal being in conflict with their issues around trust, it was like a lightbulb went off! Suddenly their life wasn't caving in around them and things made sense! They realized they were just playing out some parts of their type, and this perspective shift gave them the space to address the inequalities in their relationships and find more balance in their life. Had they not had a teacher to offer this perspective, though, they would have likely remained in that state of distress for much longer than necessary.

Our type's patterns are intricate, nuanced, and deeply unconscious; without the perspective of a trained teacher, we won't be able to see on a consistent basis the extent to which these patterns are affecting us and our lives and even how we're going about our personal and spiritual development. This perspective is absolutely vital for us to move forward, but our teachers are valuable not only because of what they see but also because of who they are.

BEING
• •

A friend once said about climbing, "Just because you *know* all the moves to do a climb doesn't mean you can actually climb it." I was immediately reminded of the mountains of self-help books I had devoured over the course of my life that had never made any sort of impact and thought to myself, "Yep, that's dead-on." Something about this statement rings deeply true for most people: we're all familiar with the trope of the book-smart teenager who lacks the ability to move through the world effectively. The nutty professor who knows all the right formulas but is somehow always creating more problems than solutions. Gurdjieff spoke to this phenomenon in his work, and having a deeper understanding of how and why it happens will drastically change how we work with the Enneagram—and also brilliantly highlights why we need a teacher.

Gurdjieff taught that just as a person grows in *knowledge*, they must also grow in *being* in order to develop true *understanding*. We know what knowledge is—it's the information we store in our brains, like $2 + 2 = 4$; the primary colors are red, blue, and yellow; the sun is a star that our planet revolves around; and so on. Being is a little harder to pin down. In some sense, being as Gurdjieff taught it could be considered what we might more commonly call virtue. I'm slightly hesitant to define being as virtue, morality, or goodness because those terms are all very charged—what they mean and look like to people is highly dependent on their own personal upbringings and experiences. Being is, in some sense, virtue, but a virtue that is universal. Being is goodness, but goodness that transcends the "right and wrong" style of thinking we're used to. Being is deeper than our personality or ego defenses; it is at the very heart of who we are. I often think of being as *how well we can actually use the information we have to the benefit of humanity*. Gurdjieff insisted on our ability as humans to "self-develop" and was focused not only on our individual liberation from our personality patterns but also on our collective liberation and movement into higher levels of understanding for the sake of our species and the cosmos. When we consider this, and understand that knowledge + being = understanding, we can see being as a much more heart-centered capacity that can be hard to define but easy to spot.

Gurdjieff gave the example of someone who was extremely intelligent but lied, cheated, and stole to make their way through the world. This person's knowledge was high, but their being was low, so their understanding was low, and they suffered because of the self-centered choices they made. Gurdjieff also mentioned someone who was kind, compassionate, and loving having a high level of being but a low level of knowledge. Their naivete led to a lower level of understanding, and they suffered because they were often taken advantage of. We need to develop both our knowledge and our being in order to move through the world effectively and reduce both our suffering and the suffering of others.

Now the question begs to be asked: How do we develop a thing that seems to be so difficult to define? Growing in knowledge is simple: hop on YouTube or instructable.com or even (*gasp*) read a book! But being is different. It's not merely a commodity that we can acquire at a moment's notice; it's something that must be shared and then cultivated and developed internally. This is why we need a teacher.

When I first began working with my yoga teacher and mentor, my life was pretty much a complete mess. My relationship was rocky at best, I had no career to speak of, and it seemed like every time I turned around, I found myself at the heart of another tragic event. I was trying to develop my-self as a yoga therapist, but I wasn't a great listener and was much too eager to show everyone around me (including my clients) how much I knew about how the world worked. As I sat with my teacher week after week, things started to shift. Sure, she has an incredible knowledge of the Yoga Sutras, the Bhagavad Gita, and the workings of the human body, but I can't say that any of those things, as helpful as they were, actually *changed* me. What really changed me was how my teacher listened to me, how she held the room when I felt like my life was spinning out, how she never seemed phased by the laundry list of ridiculous situations I got myself into, and how she gently reminded me where I needed to be putting my focus. When I sat with my teachers, there was very clearly a sharing of information and knowledge. There was (and still is), how-ever, something else—something more important—happening under the surface: a transmission of being.

To use another example, we can read books about com-passion all day long (and believe me, I have), but until we experience it firsthand, until we are on the receiving end of true compassion from someone, especially someone we've hurt or harmed in some way, we'll never be able to truly em-body it. To grow in being means to be in relationship with others. Our teachers open up spaces for us where we can ex-perience the qualities of being we want to call our own. This is what makes teachers so deeply valuable and why choosing the right teacher is so important: we will become what they are. Our being will shrink or develop because of the level of their being. This isn't merely the sharing of personality quirks, although that can happen—this is deeper. We will embody the qualities that they have, just as they did with those who taught them. This fact of the student/teacher relationship makes choosing the right teacher that much more important. If you choose a teacher who is strict, impatient, and hot-tempered (in other words, has a low level of being), you will become strict, impatient, and hot-tempered because of the being they have passed on to you. Conversely, if you work with a teacher with a high level of being—someone who is loving, kind, just, and compassionate—your being will be raised by being with them, and you will soon be more loving, kind, just, and compassionate. In the next chapter, we'll explore more in-depth what to look for in a teacher.

LINEAGE

Maybe the most important thing that we get from a qualified and experienced teacher is a *lineage*. When we become a part of a lineage, we become part of an unfolding flow that is bigger than us alone. It sometimes feels like stepping into a river. The rushing water of the generations that have gone before you are now pushing you forward. Suddenly our struggles aren't just ours, isolating us from the rest of the world; they are the same struggles that others have faced before us. We aren't easily swayed by the news of the day because what we know and experience is grounded in tradition. We are able to welcome new information and other points of view with open minds because we've seen and experienced how important it is for our understanding to develop and grow from generation to generation.

When my now wife and I had been together a little over a year, our relationship hit the rocks in a big way. I was in the middle of a difficult career transition and a major depressive episode, and she was still knee-deep in the emotional processing of her divorce. When she asked that I move out, I was heartbroken and infuriated by a request that I felt was asking too much. Luckily for me and our relationship, my spiritual director at the time had been through similar trials in his marriage and was able to not only give me the sage advice I needed but also let me know that what I was feeling was normal. He reminded me what I agreed to when I signed up for "the spiritual life." He reminded me of my spiritual lineage. He was able to show me that what my wife and I were going through was something many relationships face at some point or another and how my spiritual tradition taught that shifting my attitude could create new openings for growth and connection for both me and my wife. Had I not had his influence in my life, and thus the influence of everyone who had gone before us both in our spiritual lineage, I would have made the mistake of throwing away the best thing that has ever happened to me. Being in that lineage gave me the context I needed to make sense of a very trying situation in my life.

Being a yoga therapist, and consequently a movement professional, I see all sorts of new movement and exercise crazes pop up almost every day. From Bikram to CrossFit, from Pilates to MovNat, each of these movement modalities promises to revolutionize your body and your life. When I first started teaching yoga and being interested in working with the body, I felt myself constantly jumping from one modality to the other, which was extremely disorienting because their philosophies often contradict each other. When I started working with my teacher and investing my time and energy into yoga therapy and the viniyoga tradition, I realized that what I was missing was not the best new way to move a body but a deeper understanding of why I work with the body the way that I do. As I continued to work with my teacher and grew to understand more of the philosophy behind viniyoga, not only did I become a more effective and confident yoga therapist; I was less bothered by the revolving door of movement fads in my Instagram feed. My lineage helps me to feel more grounded in the work I do both personally and professionally.

A common experience I hear from people who are just dipping their toes into the Enneagram waters is that there seems to be so much conflicting information. Depending on which book you read or which accounts you follow on social media, you could end up with completely different information about the system and how to use it. When you don't have your own sense of lineage, it can feel nearly impossible to make sense of all the different ways people have interpreted this system. When you find a teacher and style that works for you and you commit yourself to it, though, the way is clearer. When I first encountered the Enneagram, I read Richard Rohr and Riso and Hudson, I took classes using Suzanne Stabile's curriculum, and I followed as many Instagram accounts and YouTube channels as I could. I learned a lot but still had trouble navigating all the differing approaches. When I became a part of the Enneagram community here in Austin, which is based in the Narrative Tradition, something clicked for me in a way I wasn't expecting. I knew that this was the way I wanted to both learn and teach the Enneagram. Not only did the path forward in my career become remarkably clear, but suddenly all the different approaches to the system seemed to make more sense. Once I had grounded myself in my own lineage and understood more clearly where I was coming from, I could also see more clearly where everyone else was coming from. Now, this isn't to say that when you find your lineage, you stop listening to everyone else—quite the contrary! Once you have grounded yourself in your lineage, you are able to listen more openly to what others have to say without fear of being constantly swayed by shifting thoughts and ideas. A lineage is never an excuse to insulate yourself from others but an invitation to listen more deeply.

When you are unaware of your lineage, it's easy to assume that your personal experiences are universal. Just like when you discovered the certain ways you see and respond to the world through your Enneagram type, you also discover that others see and respond to it in eight different ways. This not only makes more sense of the ways you see and respond to the world but also brings a deeper understanding to how other people operate in the world. In essence, becoming clear about your lineage is about adding context to what you know. So many times in the Enneagram world, and in life in general, our disagreements and conflicts could be short-circuited by simply having a better understanding of where both parties are coming from. When I'm unsure of where I'm coming from, or where others are coming from, it's easy to assume that I'm right and other Enneagram teachers are wrong. As I come to a deeper understanding of my lineage and the lineages of others, I can see that it's not that one of us is right and the other one is wrong but that we're simply approaching the issue from very different vantage points and trying to get very different things from it. This not only helps me clarify why I believe what I believe but also brings me to a deeper appreciation of those who disagree with me.

It's important here to note that we're all a part of many lineages, most of which we didn't choose. As we become more curious about the lineages we belong to, consciously or unconsciously, we find that some lineages are passed down by blood, like high blood pressure or the color of our skin. These lineages are biological and thus cannot be changed but in some cases can be managed and shifted. Clearly, I can't change the fact that I'm white, but I can use my inherent privilege to center more marginalized experiences. I can't help the fact that I have a family history of high cholesterol, but I can shift my diet and lifestyle to keep it from having negative effects on my health. Other lineages we find ourselves in are cultural in nature and are often passed down through family of origin, like diet or religion, and are therefore much more malleable, and we can even choose to set them down altogether (if we are aware of the depth to which they affect us, that is). Discerning between these two types of lineages can be difficult, but with some self-observation and scathing self-honesty, we can understand more of where our lineages come from and how to work with and shift them when our trajectory has us heading in a direction that is less than desirable.

I started practicing and teaching yoga at a time when what we here in the United States call "yoga" was at the height of its popularity. It had even reached the small town in Arkansas I found myself in, so clearly it was having a moment. I liked the way my body and mind felt after this specific kind of movement, and I was learning how to enjoy meditation, but most of the yogic philosophy didn't make its way into my awareness for several years. As I learned more about the history of the field I was making my career in, an interesting conversation was brewing with my peers and colleagues around the cultural appropriation of yoga. I was shocked to hear about the harm that was being done to the Indian folks who developed and sustained the traditions I was benefiting from and the ways the "yoga" I was learning had been whitewashed to be more palatable for Westerners. I was heartbroken to discover that my participation in this life-giving practice was actually perpetuating a lot of harm. For a time, I considered just dropping the whole thing. "Maybe this just isn't for me," I thought. But thanks to some wonderful teachers,* I learned that the problem wasn't just that I was a white person practicing a tradition that was developed by people who didn't look like me, but that I was unaware of how my cultural background was affecting how I engaged with what I was learning.

From there, I spent countless hours working to increase my awareness of how my cultural conditioning was affecting how I saw the world *and* seeking to learn the yogic traditions from as close to the source as I had access to. This deeply changed how I practiced and taught yoga, and I'm a better teacher and practitioner for it. By understanding that many of the concepts of yogic philosophy that directly influence the practices I was engaged in are antithetical to the way I had been trained to see things by my culture, I was able to

---

* For more on yoga teachers who are working at the intersections of yoga, social justice, and cultural identity and working through cultural appropriation, check out Susanna Barkataki at www.susannabarkataki .com and Michelle Johnson, author of *Skill in Action*, at www.michelle johnson.com.

more consciously work to build new ways of thinking about these concepts. To use the biblical analogy (calling on my own inherited religious lineage), I had to put the new wine in new wineskins. But before I could even do that, I had to realize I had an old wineskin to begin with.

When we are establishing ourselves in a new lineage, we have to engage in a certain amount of internal, and often unconscious, translating. In many ways, it can feel like learning a new language. Can you imagine attempting to learn a new language without knowing what language you were speaking to begin with? It almost hurts my brain to think about, but that's essentially what we're doing when we move into a new lineage—whether it's something like starting a yoga practice or even joining a new spiritual community—without being aware of our current lineage and how it's shaped the way we think, feel, and move through the world.

Often the Enneagram is described as a map, and to be honest, I find this metaphor extremely helpful. It can be used as a map of human personality and personal and spiritual growth, but just like any map, if we want to get anywhere, we'll also need some directions. The part most people take for granted is that for that map and those directions to be of any help at all, you'll need to know where you're starting from. Without this critical element, you'll just end up wandering in circles and most certainly *not* getting where you want to go. This is one of the most beautiful pieces of the Enneagram; it offers us the understanding that, from a personality perspective, we're starting from nine different places. We all have the same map, but because we're starting in different places, we're going to need different directions. When we take this element of the Enneagram and apply it to our greater cultural and biological backgrounds, it's easy to understand why having a better grasp of where we're starting from is so crucial.

LEARNING FROM THE FLOW

It's easy to think of our learning and growth as a personal and individual experience. We make our way through grade school and then maybe college or trade school, and we move up the ladder with little thought given to how we're obtaining all this information. The truth is that all learning, development, and growth are more like a stream, and we're simply being carried along by the flow. Our teachers teach us, as their teachers taught them, and so on back to the beginning of time. We're always a part of this flow whether we know it or not, and as you know, water always takes the path of least resistance. If we simply allow ourselves to be carried along without being aware of where we've come from or where we're going, we could very easily end up somewhere we don't like. By becoming more conscious of who has been teaching and setting examples for us and more intentional about who we choose as teachers, we can drastically change our relationship to what we're learning and create more opportunities for real, tangible, and sustainable growth. We can't always change how the river is running, but if we get out our oars and row, we can choose which side of the river we end up on.

CHAPTER 5

FINDING A GOOD TEACHER

As a member of the greater Enneagram community and a millennial, I am a part of many different online Enneagram groups. From Facebook groups to chats to message boards, the question of what the standard should be for finding a teacher comes up *all the time.* New Enneagrammers want to know who they should trust when just starting out, and many more experienced students who want to try their hand at teaching or coaching want to know if they need a piece of paper before setting up an Instagram account and creating online courses. Because the Enneagram is a very young discipline and has more of a spiritual or mystical bent than other personality typologies, the greater community has been reluctant to set or enforce any sort of rigid criteria for what it takes to be a teacher. Literally anyone can claim to be an Enneagram teacher, which makes it easy to find one (just type "Ennea" into your Instagram search bar and about 1,500 results will pop up) but hard to find the right one (or even a good one). If we're trying to find the right teacher, we need to know what to look for. While the greater community may have difficulty outlining the criteria, I, by virtue of my 8 personality type, have zero problems with it. In fact, I take great pleasure in clearing the air for anyone who may be lost in the Ennea-fog.

If you didn't notice, I made it a point to stress in the first chapter of this section that we don't just need a teacher; we need an *experienced* and *qualified* teacher. These two qualities are absolutely key for our teacher to be able to guide us effectively without their own personality getting in the way. Much in the same way Gurdjieff compared knowledge and being as two separate but complementary elements of our experience as humans, experience and qualification are the two pieces that must be fully developed for any teacher to be worth their salt. Experience and qualification are the starting points for finding a good teacher, but they won't get us all the way there. There are plenty of wonderfully experienced and qualified teachers out there who just won't work for you personally. So in addition to looking at what makes a good teacher, we'll take a long, hard look at what makes someone a good teacher *for you*.

EXPERIENCE

Most in the Enneagram world would say that experience is the most important quality in a teacher. But what do they mean by that? Am I suddenly out of the race for teacher of the year simply because I've only been doing it a few years compared to other teachers' few decades? Some may think so, but what I've found in my personal life as well as in the lives of people I've had the privilege to study under is that experience is more than just a running tally of years. Yes, how long a person has been working in the profession certainly is something to be mindful of, but it's not always a deal-breaker. The most important part of experience in terms of choosing a teacher actually has less to do with how long they've been working as a teacher and more to do with how long—and how well—they've been *working on themselves.*

A few summers ago, I was working with a client who was struggling with their sexual orientation and gender identity. It was clear from our first session together that this was something that weighed heavily on them, and with good reason. Coming from a deeply conservative and fundamentalist Christian background, they had been steeped in purity culture and as a result carried a lot of shame and grief around their sexual experiences and desires and had no framework or vocabulary for dealing with how they were coming to understand their own gender identity. When working with my clients on not only issues of gender identity and sexuality but also how they intersect with a fundamentalist Christian upbringing, I draw heavily on my own lived experience. I don't believe that because I lived through it (or more rightly, something similar to it), I have the magic key. But I do believe that because of the way I faced my own struggle with these issues, I have a deep respect for the gravity of the situation. I was able to create and hold more space for my client because of the space I allowed my experience of coming to terms with my queerness to create in me. This space allowed my client the room to really explore, and feel safe exploring, what felt so dangerous to look at for so long.

When thinking about how experienced a teacher is, we ought to shift our thinking from quantitative to qualitative, from "how long?" to "how well?" Our lived experiences, if met well, create in us the space to see the world and those we interact with more compassionately. No amount of training and no number of years doing a certain kind of work can give us this same space. Real experience comes from the work we've done on ourselves and the way we have handled what life has dealt us. My coming out process was a time of immense growth for me both when I came out as queer and then again years later when I came out as nonbinary. Coming out as queer in a small town in Arkansas while living with my highly religious and conservative family taught me the value of community and living authentically and openly. While I was resistant at first, I ended up welcoming the experience with a vulnerable and open heart, which was a scary and challenging thing to do. Years later, working through my own gender identity, things moved more slowly and cautiously. I learned the value of being gentle with myself and cultivated the ability to listen more closely to the subtle experiences I was having, both big points of growth for someone leading with type 8. Both of these experiences deeply changed me, making me a more compassionate person. Now, had I met both of these experiences and opted out of the growth and development they offered me in favor of a more comfortable or "easier" path, not only would I have missed out on the opportunity to grow, but I wouldn't have the space those experiences created in me to offer my clients.

Of course, the question of "how long?" isn't completely irrelevant—someone who is twenty-five would have far fewer opportunities for these kinds of experiences than someone who is fifty. But we have to remember that just because someone has been given the invitation to grow doesn't mean they showed up to the party. We have to be mindful of and balance both "How long?" and "How well?" when considering who we will have as our teacher. Now, in asking "How well?" we aren't looking for someone who's always gotten it right; we're looking for someone who can be open and honest about how they've gotten things wrong, someone who's been willing to take the more dangerous and uncomfortable path that growth offers. For those who have a tendency to be straitlaced, their path to growth may be a willingness to take risks. For those who have been more impulsive, it may be the willingness to move more slowly and thoughtfully. Good teachers are failures! Good teachers are those who have made mistakes and met their failure with humility and a willingness to learn. The experiences that teachers have throughout their lives and their willingness to use them as tools for growing in compassion and understanding are what make them good teachers.

QUALIFICATION

It's important for our teachers to be not only *experienced* but also *qualified*. Calling a teacher qualified means that they have put themselves through a process of training and refinement. It means they've gained specific skills that make them better at their jobs, and most importantly, it means they've made a conscious decision to become an active part of their own lineage—they have their own teacher or teachers.

The kind of teacher we're talking about might not have a degree in education. They might be a spiritual director or a therapist; they may be a life coach or a yoga teacher. The qualifications that would make someone a good teacher are varied. I've had several different teachers throughout my life: one was a minister and spiritual director; a few were yoga teachers. I had a life coach who was also a Theta healer as a guide for a few years. One of my most impactful teachers was a musician who had a day job working at Kmart. The point I'm trying to make here is that when we're trying to find a good teacher, the *kind* of qualification matters less than the fact that they have it. A little farther in this chapter, we'll discuss situations in which the kind of qualification does matter, but for now it's important to remember that teachers come in all shapes, sizes, and qualifications.

In my twenties, the running joke with several of my friends was that I was their own personal life coach. I liked listening to my friends. Somehow, I could always see something they couldn't, and I was all too happy to tell them what it was. Years later, though, when I decided to actually become a yoga therapist and an Enneagram coach, I knew I needed to be "official." So I went through the proper avenues and not only became a certified yoga therapist with the International Association of Yoga Therapists but also became a certified Enneagram teacher with the Narrative Enneagram.

A piece of paper or a certification doesn't really mean anything on its own, but the hope behind all certifications and degrees is that the person who obtains them has undergone a specific kind of growth process—that they are now different, and ideally more skilled, than they were before. These new skills are the first reason that a teacher needs to be qualified and not just experienced. While I served as a pretty decent "life coach" to my friends when I was younger, the skills I learned through my various training processes

allowed me to actually do the job well. I learned how to better hold space for people and allow the work we were doing
to be client centered. I learned tools for dealing with physical and psycho-emotional issues as well as trauma-informed
care. There is, of course, a lot to be said about a person's
natural talent at a given job, but without the proper training
and skill building, talent or experience alone is not enough.

The second reason a teacher needs to be qualified and
not just experienced is because the qualification process
sets the standard. Let's take medical doctors, for example.
How often do you ask for your doctor's GPA? I know I never
have. That's because even the ones who didn't get straight
A's have still undergone enough of an educational and transformational process that we've decided as a society that we
can trust them with our health and well-being. Basically,
if they've gone through the process, they are at least *good
enough*. We tend to think that someone's qualifications or
degrees tell just how great they are at their job, but the reality is that they only tell us *how bad they aren't*, and this is
actually an incredibly valuable piece of information. When
looking for a teacher, their certifications don't tell us how
good they're going to be as teachers or guides in our personal and spiritual journey, but they do show us the baseline
of what they will be capable of because of their training.
This starts to narrow the playing field somewhat and lowers
the possible risk of starting out with a new teacher. Someone who isn't qualified could be completely capable—or they
could be absolutely terrible, anywhere between 0 percent and
100 percent. A qualified teacher may not be 100 percent,
but they also won't be lower than 50 percent. We can't gauge
their experience from their business cards or even the initial

meeting, but knowing their qualifications helps us have a better sense of their basic skill levels.

Maybe the most important part of a teacher's qualification for our purposes is that in choosing to undergo the process of qualification, the teacher has become an active participant in their own lineage and therefore can help us become an active participant in ours as well. I always tell people looking for their own teacher that they need to know who their teacher's teacher is, and the farther back you can go, the better. I am an active part in two specific lineages: one in the yoga world and one in the Enneagram world. In the yoga world, I'm the student of Amanda Green, who is a student of Chase Bossart, who was a student of T. K. V. Desikachar, who created the viniyoga tradition in India after synthesizing the teachings of his own teachers. In the Enneagram world, the lines are a little less clean, but I'm a student of Lesley and Rick Bradstreet as well as Renée Rosario, Peter O'Hanrahan, Terri Saracino, and Marion Gilbert, all of whom are the students of Helen Palmer (who I have also had the honor of studying with) and Dr. David Daniels, who were students of Kathleen Speeth and Claudio Naranjo, who was a student of Oscar Ichazo, who was a student of Gurdjieff. In both cases, I can trace what I'm learning back to the people who developed the school of thought to begin with. I can see who influenced whom and how the disciplines have changed, developed, and unfolded through the generations.

Growing up in a Christian household and diving deep into my own expression of faith in my teens, I committed myself to memorizing as much of the Bible as my tiny, undeveloped brain could possibly hold. Memory verses, anyone? I was super into them. What I always had trouble with, though, were the parts in the Bible that listed names much like I did in the last paragraph. Abraham begot Isaac, Isaac begot Jacob who became Israel, who begot etc., etc., etc. I didn't get why I needed to know all these "begots," and honestly, they were frustrating! Who cares? It wasn't until I started to really understand my own need for a lineage that all these "begots" started to make sense. Understanding where we come from in either a biological or educational sense helps give us a sense of context and direction. As I mentioned in the last chapter, it helps ground us, and if we want to be grounded, we certainly want our teachers to be grounded as well. Understanding where they're coming from gives us a better sense of where they're headed and if that's somewhere we want to go too.

Before I chose to become a certified teacher with the Narrative Enneagram, I had researched basically every Enneagram certification process I could find. I found a lot of programs that were clearly very well designed and whose alumni I deeply respected, and I also found a lot of programs that were extremely shady—the Enneagram equivalent of diploma mills. I ended up choosing the Narrative Enneagram for two main reasons. First was that it was reputable, founded by two giants in the Enneagram world. It was clearly the real deal. But as I mentioned before, there are a lot of reputable schools. The other thing that helped me make the decision was that I resonated with the *way* they taught—it was clear to me that this was the specific *flow* I wanted to be a part of. I wanted to be a part of the lineage the Narrative Enneagram is building. So when people are looking for a teacher, and they know they like the way the Narrative Enneagram works, and they see "Certified Narrative Enneagram Teacher" after my name, they know what lineage I'm a part of, and this helps us answer the next big question.

WHAT MAKES A GOOD TEACHER *FOR YOU*?

Without a doubt, there are thousands of qualified and experienced Enneagram teachers in the world who would all be considered "good" or even "great" by the standards I've set forth in this chapter, but very few of them would be considered a "good" or "great" teacher for *you* specifically. Maybe you've had the experience of finding a new service provider, or a doctor, or a therapist, who came very highly recommended by friends and family, but after the first few visits, it became clear this person was *not* for you. It had nothing to do with their experience or their qualifications—they could be absolutely stellar, but something just didn't work for you. This can be an especially frustrating experience. So now that we've narrowed down what it means for a person to be a good teacher generally, it's time to explore what it means for someone to be a good teacher on a more particular and personal level.

Are You Going My Way?

One of the first questions we have to answer when finding a teacher is "Have they been where I want to go?" Answering this question is where a teacher's specific qualification becomes more important. In other words, to reuse an analogy from a previous chapter, if you want to learn how cars work, you would probably do well to find a mechanic you can apprentice under, while a therapist or a spiritual

director may be less helpful. Conversely, if you were looking to find more fulfillment and meaning in your life, the
mechanic would most likely not be able to get you very far,
and a therapist, coach, or spiritual director would be much
more effective. From there you can begin to get even more
specific. Say you want to work on cars—but not just any
cars. You want to work specifically on classic American-
made muscle cars. This means you would want to find
not just any mechanic, but a mechanic who specializes in
American muscle cars. Let's say you've just embarked on
your spiritual journey, and while you've spent most of your
life socialized in Christian traditions, you've recently been
inspired by Buddhism. Finding a spiritual director or spiritual teacher in the Buddhist tradition will get you where you
want to go, but finding someone with experience in both
Buddhist and Christian traditions will be even more effective because they will be able to help you bridge the gap
between the two traditions.

When I first moved to Austin, Texas, my girlfriend at the
time and I were looking for a church home. I was also interested in finding a mentor or spiritual director. I had grown
up in the Christian church and left it in a fury my senior year
of high school. I spent nearly a decade outside of any church
environment but still considered myself a spiritual seeker.
After having my life changed by yoga while living in Arkansas, though, I found myself sitting in an Episcopal church
week after week because my yoga teacher was the wife of
the priest. When it came time to move to Texas, I was hungry for something that fed me spiritually where I was but
also honored my Christian roots. When I first walked into
the Church of Conscious Harmony (CCH), it felt like home.

They read scripture and followed the lectionary (a three-year cycle of scripture readings shared by many Christian denominations), but they also actively practiced meditation and spoke of the unity of the cosmos. The minister, Tim, spoke in a way that felt open and expansive, a far cry from the close-minded faith of my youth. I was soon sitting with Tim for spiritual direction whenever I could get on his schedule. Tim had spent time in India studying with a guru before coming back to the United States to be ordained, and he was also a devout student of Gurdjieff and P. D. Ouspensky. He had already been where I was wanting to go, so he was an ideal teacher for me and offered invaluable guidance for the three years I was his student. He was able to speak to me in a language that really resonated with me because of his past experiences, and this created the next important aspect in finding a teacher.

The "Click"

One essential quality in a teacher who's right for you is the "click" or the "vibe." Basically, do you feel connected to this person? Do you feel inspired? Do the two of you speak the same language? Being able to "click" with your teacher is the most important element in finding the right teacher for you. Without this click and connection, you won't experience the deeper flow and unfolding that's happening. It's this click that enables us to trust our teacher, and trust is absolutely vital in the teacher/student relationship. If we can't trust the person we're asking to help us see our blind spots, what's the point of asking in the first place? This trust comes at different paces for different people, but the trust never comes unless the "click" is already there.

As a guitarist, I was mostly self-taught, but when I finally got around to enrolling in college, I was determined to take advantage of the music department's wonderful teachers. Their guitar teacher was, for lack of a better term, a total badass. A jazz guitar virtuoso who had toured with many of the greats, he'd been teaching at this university for several years. Watching him play was mesmerizing. When I finally got a slot on his schedule for guitar lessons, I was sure it would be like getting struck by lightning! I just knew I was going to improve so much in no time; this guy was just too good! Spoiler alert—that's not what happened. To be honest, for a long time, I wasn't even really sure what happened, but it wasn't lightning, that's for sure. My progress moved at a snail's pace if it moved at all. It just didn't make sense. This teacher was an amazing musician and an incredible teacher. He had the experience and the qualifications, and he clearly had been to all the places I wanted to go, but we just didn't click. Now, it's easy to look at a situation like this and want to point fingers or try to troubleshoot. Maybe I wasn't a good enough student, or maybe he felt uncomfortable teaching womxn (I still identified as a woman at the time), but the truth is that we just didn't click—and that's OK.

From the perspective of a teacher working with clients, one of the first things the pros will tell you is to work with people who fit with you and your style. People in my line of work aim to have the freedom to only work with clients who we click with, to have the freedom to say, "I'm sorry, I don't think we're a good fit." This ineffable "fit" or "click" is what takes all the competition out of being a coach or therapist. We're not trying to hoover up everyone in our market; we're trying to make ourselves available to the people we're meant to work with. Qualified and experienced teachers know that a lack of click isn't a problem to be fixed, and you should know it too. Just because you don't click with a teacher doesn't mean they're a bad teacher, and it certainly doesn't mean you're a bad student. It simply means the two of you aren't meant to work together, and there's someone different out there for both of you.

Maybe the hardest part about finding someone you click with is the fact that it can take some time to feel out. In some cases, the lack of click is clear from the start—you know before you even finish shaking hands that this isn't going to work out. But more often than not, both the teacher and the client need to undertake an exploratory period where we're just trying to figure things out. I've always been a quick judge of character. So as both a student and a teacher, I rarely have trouble feeling out whether I click with someone. Many of my clients, though, don't have the same quick sense of certainty. One client of mine took longer than most to really settle in and trust that the click was there. While I could tell pretty quickly that we had the right chemistry, she was in the midst of a lot of personal struggle, and getting help was both a deeply challenging and vulnerable process. She had been to several other specialists, therapists, and coaches, and no one was able to help her move forward (yoga therapists are often a last-ditch effort when nothing else has helped), so her reluctance toward me made a lot of sense. Despite her reluctance, she never missed a session and worked hard to incorporate the practices and routines we developed into her daily life. Soon things in her life started to shift, and she was able to fully embrace the therapeutic relationship we had been building over the past several months. Feeling out the click can take time, and I think we often do ourselves and our teachers a disservice by not giving them more of a chance, but as my client showed, there are things we can do to ensure we've given ourselves and our potential teachers the best possible shot at real change and growth, which we'll explore in the next chapter.

STARTING THE SEARCH

Finding a teacher can feel like a daunting process, but it can be helpful to understand that your perfect teacher is actually out there looking for you too. As a yoga therapist and coach, a large chunk of my time is spent on making sure the right people can find me because I *really* want to find them! Of course, I want to be a helpful resource to everyone who knocks on my door (or messages me on Instagram) regardless of whether we're a good fit for the student/teacher relationship. Like many if not all people in my line of work, I've built an extensive referral network: people I know and trust who work in a variety of different ways and have a variety of what we like to call "ideal clients." This means that if someone who starts working with me isn't a good fit for nearly any reason, I can at the very least point them in the direction of someone who I believe would be a better fit. To be honest, I don't know any teacher who meets all the aforementioned criteria who doesn't have this kind of network, so even if you strike out on your first try in finding a teacher, you'll be at least one step closer to hitting it out of the park with the teacher who's right for you.

In an attempt to help make this process even easier for you, I've made a list of incredible teachers you can get in touch with in the "Resources" section of the appendix. Start googling and sending emails, or even making phone calls if you're that brave, and soon you'll be building the transformative and healing relationship you need to take you deeper into your own personal Enneagram work.

CHAPTER 6

BEING A GOOD STUDENT

I've been on both sides of the search for a new teacher. I've been the student or client hoping that this is the last set of intake paperwork I have to fill out, and I've been the coach trying to understand the crux of a client's issues as quickly as humanly possible to keep them sticking around. It can be an incredibly strange dynamic. Sometimes it feels like both parties are putting on a show, trying to get the other to like them or approve of them. Sometimes one or both parties can be standoffish, as if the whole thing is some sort of audition process. As we saw in the last chapter, an experienced and qualified teacher has been trained to be aware of themselves and how what they bring into a room will shift the dynamic. But it's just as important for us as clients to understand that how we show up in the first few sessions with our prospective teachers can really change what happens too.

A couple of years before I started the process to become a yoga therapist and Enneagram coach, I was in a place in my life where I felt like I couldn't get enough help. I had just gone through a breakup, I was having doubts about my current career choice (slinging coffee every morning was starting to get old), and I just generally felt pretty crappy. During this time, I was trying out teachers like someone might try on shoes in their local department store. Everyone from yoga teachers to Reiki practitioners, spiritual directors to therapists, Theta healers to business coaches, I left no stone unturned! In the midst of all the frenzy I was feeling, I didn't create very deep relationships with these teachers. I felt a sense of urgency about finding the right person or thing to "fix" my issues, to make sense of things for me, and to tell me exactly what to do to get things "right" the next go-around. I can see now, several years later, that in my hurry, I was missing out on a lot of what each one of these coaches and teachers had to offer me. I ended up sticking with a life coach who, quite honestly, was a lot like me. She also identified as a type 8 and was interested in the directive and action-oriented nature of coaching, which of course I loved. I feel fortunate that I was able to build such a wonderfully enriching relationship with her. I know that she was the right person at the right time, and as I look back, I can see how much of what I was unconsciously bringing into the room prevented me from seeing the value in the other teachers I had initial sessions with. Had I been more self-aware at the time, or even just less desperate, I could have seen how my type was playing into my search for a teacher and could have chosen a different approach that would have led to a deeper experience.

Of course, it's rarely helpful to play the "what if" game, but the point still stands: starting out with a new teacher can be a difficult process and requires a lot from both the teacher and the student. As students, we have to fill teachers in on our history, get them caught up on all the things we've been dealing with, continually remind them of our dog's name so they don't get her confused with our partner or spouse. It's a lot, and even if the teacher is great, the onboarding process can be difficult. Any pressure we put on ourselves or the prospective teacher can make it hard for us to observe ourselves clearly and make the process even more difficult. This difficulty can often cloud our judgment and make it nearly impossible to discern if this is the right person for us. But there are a few things we can do on our end to make this process run more smoothly and continue to benefit the relationship long after the onboarding is over.

There's that old saying when people are looking for an intimate partnership: "It's not about finding the right person; it's about being the right person." While I believe it's really more of a balance between these two things, the saying brings up a really important point that we often overlook: the way we show up in a relationship plays a part in how the relationship unfolds. The same is true in our teacher/student relationships. If we, as students, can show up, listen well, and try everything on— basically, be good students—then we give our teachers the best opportunity to be good teachers.

SHOWING UP
• •

This may seem like a no-brainer, but showing up is more than just a physical act. Of course showing up definitely means keeping the appointments you schedule with your teacher—you actually need to be there!—but showing up is also about how present we are with our teachers when we're in the room (or on the video call, or whatever) with them and how much of ourselves we bring to the sessions.

I had a client for a short time who saw me online from her home. She was a stay-at-home mom with small children, and nearly every session we had to pause what we were doing so she could address some issue with her children. Every time this happened, it caused a rupture in the container we were trying to build, and even though we had several sessions, we weren't able to move forward in the way we might have if she'd been able to prioritize herself, set aside distraction- or kid-free time, and be truly present during our time together. Please don't read this as any sort of attack on stay-at-home moms (or dads or other kinds of parents). The same sort of issue could arise with a client who couldn't turn off their phone during sessions or someone who is consistently late to sessions. When we aren't present, physically or otherwise, we rob ourselves of the opportunity to build a positive and healing relationship with our teacher. If we aren't able to keep our attention with what's happening for us and our teacher in the room, we're more likely to simply repeat our unhelpful relational patterns with our teacher, which greatly limits how we will be able to grow in the context of the relationship. If we want something different, we need to bring more presence to all our relationships, especially the one we build with our teacher.

Another kind of showing up can be a little harder to fully embody because it requires us to decompartmentalize ourselves and let someone see all of us. I had been working with my teacher for more than a year when I started working through issues with my gender identity. It was a grueling process (and, honestly, still is at times), and while I needed support, I didn't talk to my teacher openly about it for a long time. I justified this by minimizing the situation and claiming that it wasn't that big of a deal and that it clearly wasn't affecting the issues my teacher and I were working on (spoiler alert, it was a big deal and was most definitely affecting all my issues). When I finally went through the process of explaining all I had been discovering about myself and working on, my teacher was able to help me see more clearly the connections between my gender identity and all the other things we had been focusing on. With this new insight, our work together progressed rapidly, and regardless of the speed of our work, I felt more supported and cared for in a situation where I had previously felt very alone.

We can't expect our teachers to do their best work if they only know half the story. Now, sure, we don't have to lay everything about ourselves bare the very first time we meet someone—the trust we're building with them takes time. We have to keep in mind, though, that the more we show up as our whole selves, the easier our teacher can help us make sense of it all. So whether it's a matter of showing up on time, staying focused, or bringing your full self to the table, if you aren't showing up fully, you can't expect to get much out of your time with even the best teacher.

A big part of showing up is being honest. It doesn't matter how present we are if we're not being honest and clear when we work with our teacher. This kind of honesty is hard, and we as a society don't have a lot of practice with it. The honesty I'm talking about is less an avoidance of telling all-out lies and more in the subtle interactions we have on a daily basis. For example, think about how you answer the question "How are you doing?" We've been trained cultur-ally that there are only a few acceptable answers, and this training spills into every interaction in our lives, whether we like it or not. When this kind of patterning comes into play with our teachers, we lose valuable time and insight because of our inability to speak truthfully.

No one is a mind reader, and our personal teacher, mentor, or therapist isn't a magician. When you engage in this kind of work, having open and honest communication is vitally im-portant. Your teacher may ask you to do something that doesn't work for you—you may try it on and realize it doesn't fit. If you aren't honest about this, about your experience of what's happening, your teacher won't have the information they need to direct you effectively. Most of us have a tendency to cover up the negative aspects of our lives when interacting with new people, but the same can be true of the positive aspects. Just as we've been conditioned to only answer with a select few phrases when asked how we're doing, we've also been condi-tioned to assume there is always something wrong in our lives. If we are consistently only sharing what is wrong in our world with our teacher, our teacher will be at the same disadvantage they would be at if we were sugarcoating everything.

Developing honest communication sets a precedent and helps us build a more honest relationship with ourselves and everyone around us. Honesty of this kind is calibrating; it allows us to see more clearly and respond more appropri-ately to the situations of our lives. When we are truly honest with ourselves and those around us, we are more likely to actually receive what we need from others and have a clearer path forward for ourselves. The value of this kind of honesty can't be overstated in the student/teacher relationship. Often the biggest issue in preventing this kind of honesty, though, is our type structure. The way we respond and communicate with others is heavily influenced by our types, so one of the first things we can do is start being aware of how our type is affecting our communication. As a 4, are you overfocusing on the negative and dramatic? As a 7, are you only capable of sharing the silver linings and keeping the dark clouds out of view? Now, these are very stereotypical examples, but they help point us to the practice of checking in with ourselves as we're sharing with others, especially our teachers. How much is your type playing into your ability to be truly honest? Asking this question deeply and seeking the real answer will put you on the fast track toward this transformative honesty.

LISTENING WELL

Of course, if we want to build a strong relationship with our teacher, we need to listen to them, but listening well is much more nuanced than we usually anticipate. There are two parts to listening well because there are two people in the student/teacher relationship. Yes, we have to be able to listen to, and really hear, what our teachers are saying to us, but we also have to be able to listen to and hear what's coming up for us in response.

In my first-ever therapy session, I sat down on a comfy couch across from a kind-looking blonde woman and explained that I was experiencing a lot of really high highs and really low lows emotionally. I promptly followed up that statement by informing my new therapist that I didn't want to focus on mellowing out the highs, but I wanted to make sure I wasn't having these deeply low lows. Basically, just give me the good stuff, and I'll pass on all that depression stuff. I had pretty much made up my mind, so when my therapist tried to explain the manic/depressive cycle, and how properly managing the highs helps prevent the lows, I wasn't interested in hearing it. It would take me a solid three years before I allowed this lesson to sink in. The places where I had "made up my mind," the places where I felt particularly defensive, prevented me from hearing the message I really needed. Similarly, a friend told me about how she was starting with a new teacher (because her last one pressed too hard on a stalwart belief she was defending vigorously). Shortly after, she was finding yet another teacher after only a few sessions—because of the same problem.

It's important to temper these examples with an understanding that our teachers aren't always right, but if we're holding onto thoughts and beliefs so tightly that we aren't able to even entertain something that conflicts with them, we're limiting our ability to relate not only to our teacher but also to everyone around us. We all have some deeply dogmatic beliefs that we're guarding. Maybe you're a dyed-in-the-wool Republican or Democrat or Independent. Maybe you believe that you're an awful person who makes terrible mistakes (looking at you, 1s), or maybe you believe that you're secretly a superhero who doesn't need to care for themselves in the same way mere mortals do (where are my 8s at?). Whatever these beliefs are, the more defensive and guarded we are about them, the more likely they're limiting our ability to experience the growth and transformation we're craving. Holding our beliefs more lightly doesn't mean we let go of all of them altogether; sometimes we believe things born out of our own experience that are meaningful and helpful in our journey toward growth. But when these beliefs become absolutes and nonnegotiables in our lives, we cut ourselves off from the incoming flow of information and get stuck where we are. Being able to listen to our teachers, even when we might not like what they're saying, keeps us connected to that flow and keeps us moving in the right direction.

Just as important as listening to our teachers, however, is listening to ourselves. If we hang on every word that falls out of our teacher's mouth but can't "hear" our own experience, then we won't know if the direction our teacher is leading us in is right. In an interview I did with Chase Bossart for my podcast, *Conscious Construction*, he told a story that his teacher, T. K. V. Desikachar, told him about finding a teacher. Mr. Desikachar had a saying, "When you are looking for a teacher, keep both eyes open," suggesting that we could find a teacher nearly anywhere if we're truly open to it, but the saying continued, "When you find your teacher, keep one eye open." This piece always stood out to me. It's the perfect metaphor for allowing ourselves to be open and trust another person to guide us without fully surrendering our autonomy. We have to not only keep an eye on and pay attention to what our teacher is telling and showing us; we must also keep one eye on how we are taking in and experiencing everything. When we can find the balance between these two, we'll be looking and listening on a much deeper level.

TRYING EVERYTHING ON

This may be the hardest part of not only finding a good teacher but sticking with one. I had just finished outlining this chapter and wrote "Try Everything On" almost as an afterthought, and I thought to myself, "Oooh, that's a good one." Slightly proud of myself, I folded up my laptop, shoved it in my backpack, and headed to my session with my teacher. I sat in front of her and shared the struggles I was facing at the time—mostly not having enough energy and having big mood swings. She then asked me about my diet. What was I eating? When was I eating it? Admittedly, I had plenty of room for improvement in how I ate. Too much eating out, almost zero regularity in my schedule, and a gnarly queso habit (if you live anywhere near a Torchy's Tacos, you'll understand) all made for a perfect storm that was affecting both my budget and my health. Of course, I had all the excuses: "I'm just too busy!" "It's not that bad!" "Who has time to cook now, anyway?" My teacher cut right through all of it and zeroed in on my very 8ish habits of denial and self-neglect and suggested that I spend more time actually making food for myself. To say I was resistant would be an extreme understatement. I told her there in the moment that I didn't want to do it. It seemed pointless—impossible, even! There was just no way, and I just didn't want to!

And then the irony hit me like a ton of bricks. Hadn't I just written down that trying things on was part of the process? "Ugh, fine," I thought to myself. Luckily, my teacher wasn't upset in the least and really allowed me to take my journey at my own pace. As the days passed, and I made small shifts here and there in my schedule and my food choices, I realized how right she was and how much better I felt just taking this time to care for and nourish myself. After only a few days, I could feel a vast improvement in my moods and physical well-being. At first, I was nervous

I wouldn't be able to make any change, but soon I had the energy and capacity to completely shift my diet to something truly nourishing. Over time, my fatigue and mood swings lessened, and I started feeling like myself again. It was clear my teacher was right on, and if I hadn't challenged my initial resistance and tried on what she had suggested, I would still be stuck in that particular pattern of not caring for myself and feeling crappy because of it.

A teacher is someone who will challenge us. They will push us to places that we don't really want to go because they're leading us past what's comfortable into what is truly transformational. If we want to experience this transformation, we must be willing to at least try on what our teachers suggest for us. Of course, not everything we try on will truly fit, and that's where this trying on must be balanced with our ability to listen well, to really show up for ourselves and our teacher, and to be honest. When we can do all these things, we will be the kind of students who can build a truly transformational relationship with our teachers and grow in tangible, meaningful, and sustainable ways.

DON'T DIG TOO MANY WELLS

As I discussed in the last chapter, it's important to be specific about what we want and find a teacher who is experienced and qualified in the areas that we want to focus on in our lives as well as with the tools that we hope to use. Often that mindset can lead us to seek out different teachers for all the areas of our lives and different kinds of tools we want to use, and if we aren't careful, we'll end up with a slew of teachers whose guidance and direction are in conflict with one another. Even when we're being excellent students by following all of the aforementioned guidelines, our growth could still end up stunted if we're getting input from too many sources.

Remember that frenzied time in my life I described at the beginning of this chapter? During that time, I found myself in this exact kind of position. I had developed a strong relationship with my life coach, and her insight into my life was extremely valuable. At the same time, I was in the process of deepening my relationship with my spiritual director, who also happened to be the minister of my church. I was also discovering my love and passion for the Enneagram and was spending a lot of time soaking up as much information as I could about the system and how my type was affecting my life. On top of all of that, I spent time with a Reiki practitioner and a spiritual and energetic healer who practiced shamanism. Oh, and there was also the light bath and crystal singing bowl sessions I did! Basically, in true 8 fashion, when I had set my sights on "healing," I was determined to address it from all angles—I was going to heal every part of my self and heal it right then! Soon, though, I found myself confused at how to integrate all that I was learning and experiencing. I was being pulled in several different directions. One teacher said to do this, the other said to do that, and it was too much for me to take in. I was missing out on the real value of what each was sharing with me.

One of the other gems of wisdom that Chase Bossart shared with my yoga therapy class was this: "Don't dig too many wells." He explained that working with a teacher was a lot like digging a well. When we dig a well, we engage with some difficult work, and often some length of time needs to pass before we start to reap the deep and transformative benefits. If we're spending our time developing relationships with too many teachers, we're essentially digging too many wells. Instead of having one (or maybe two) really deep wells that provide us with what we're really wanting and needing in order to grow, we end up with a handful of shallow wells that can't provide us with anything of substance. This will undoubtedly leave us feeling dry and thirsty.

The exact number of teachers who actually support each of us in our journeys will differ. Some of us will only want one, while others can comfortably manage three or four (looking at you, 7s!) and still create a sense of depth and meaning with each one. I will admit that I also find a lot of value in developing a relationship with another teacher aside from my main one when I understand that it's only for a season. The real key to managing these relationships is prioritizing. When something one teacher says is in conflict with what another says, who do we listen to? Who do we prioritize? These are very important questions to answer anytime we're working with more than one teacher.

When I was launching my business, I got a business coach who helped me get things off the ground and get myself organized. Her insight and direction were absolutely invaluable to me, and I can honestly say I wouldn't be writing this book right now if it weren't for her. But as valuable as this relationship was, I knew that it was only going to be for a short time. I also knew that if what she was asking me to do ever conflicted with what my main teacher was asking of me, I would have to put it to the side. Making these priorities clear when we're working with more than one teacher will help keep us steady when it starts to feel like we're getting lost in a storm of conflicting messages.

A NOTE TO THE TYPES

I see a lot of people in the Enneagram community looking for teachers or therapists or coaches and using that person's type as some sort of criterion to be met or checked off. "I'm a 6, so I definitely can't have an 8 teacher," or "I'm a 1, so a 1 therapist is the only person who could understand." This is not only a bad way to go about finding a teacher; it's also a gross misuse of the Enneagram. There are plenty of things to consider when finding a teacher, but the teacher's type is not one of them. That being said, there are things that each of the types should consider about themselves and their prospective teacher as they move into this new relationship.

Type 1: You may initially look for a teacher who can be as precise and strict as you aspire to be yourself, but one of the most important things for your journey of growth is the ability to be gentle with yourself and others. Finding a teacher who will cut you some slack and model what self-acceptance looks like for you, while you may hate the idea at first, will support you in your own journey toward serenity.

Type 2: Everyone needs an experienced and qualified teacher to help us on our path, even you! The teacher/student relationship can be a great place for you to practice letting someone see you in your neediness and accepting their help. Be mindful of your tendency to play off your real feelings to focus on someone else, and remember that your teacher is here to help you, not the other way around. A teacher who holds strong personal and emotional boundaries will be your best guide toward transformation.

Type 3: One of the most important things the teacher/student relationship offers us is accountability. Make sure you're not turning your accountability into an audience. Audiences only want to see us when we're "on it," but for your teacher to hold you accountable, they have to be able to see all of you, including where you feel like you've "failed." Remember that there are no shortcuts to enlightenment. A teacher who moves slowly, takes their time, and encourages you to do the same will be leading you in the right direction.

Type 4: Remember what they say: "After the ecstasy, the laundry." A lot of this journey can feel extremely mundane, and a teacher who helps you lean into that is someone who can help you truly see the beauty in every moment. Your tendency to overemotionalize every situation keeps you stuck, so don't focus so much on how you feel about your teacher from moment to moment, but keep your focus on the plan of action.

Type 5: The best way to know if a teacher is right for you is to meet with the teacher. Don't allow yourself to get caught up in the researching; just book a consultation. Your experience will tell you more than anyone's website ever could. Teachers who are more emotionally focused and can help you incorporate embodiment practices will offer you more than the intellectual experts you may find yourself unconsciously gravitating toward.

Type 6: It can be especially tempting for you to seek out the absolute authority in a teacher, but a teacher who continues to point you back to yourself and your experience will point you in the right direction every time. A teacher who is experienced with physical practices can help you focus the mind and calm the nervous system—the more grounded your teacher, the better!

Type 7: If we really knew what we were signing up for when we started this journey, none of us would have been interested—but the true freedom you're hungering for is waiting for you on the other side of all of this hard (and boring!) work. Don't give up on your teacher too soon! This relationship gives you the opportunity to practice the patience and commitment you need to experience the real magic this life has to offer. Look for a teacher who can help you slow down and take life one step at a time.

Type 8: I get it, you don't like being told what to do. But take a breath (or ten) and allow yourself to try it on. It's important for you to find a teacher who won't balk when you put up a fight, but don't fall into the trap of believing that just because a person won't fight with you means that what they say isn't valuable. A teacher who leads you back toward your heart is leading you toward your growth (even if it seems like a bunch of mushy nonsense at first).

Type 9: Finding your "no" is often the first step in truly finding your "yes." A teacher who invites you to disagree will absolutely change your life. The teacher/student relationship is a great place for you to practice setting and sticking to your boundaries. Don't forget that your anger is the fire you need to change your life. It's important to find a teacher who can help you not only uncover your anger but also hold your anger well.

NO TEACHER IS PERFECT

It doesn't matter if you're the best student ever and if you've found the most wonderful teacher—no teacher is perfect or even a "perfect" fit, and no teacher/student relationship is immune to the pitfalls of this particular kind of relating. The Enneagram's lineage is fraught with rifts between teachers and their students. I don't take this as a vote against developing these kinds of relationships but instead as a signal that we need to develop another part of our stool in order to stay balanced. Just as having a teacher helps us keep our personal practices in check, developing intentional and Conscious Community can take the pressure off our student/teacher relationship. In the next section of this book, we'll discuss the concept of community, how it balances our three-legged stool, and how to move into it with intention.

LEG III

COMMUNITY

CHAPTER 7

THE POWER OF COMMUNITY

At this point in the book, I feel like you know me pretty well. I've shared a lot of myself in the pages of this book, and I feel like I can be really honest with you. So here's me being completely honest: I've dreaded writing this section of the book from the moment I wrote the outline. Not because I don't think it's important, or because I feel like it was going to be a drag, but because I knew, even then, what it was going to require of me. In order to write this, I knew that I had to fully show up in community. And not just any community—my community, my conscious and intentional community that served as the springboard for me in my career, personal life, and spiritual journey. And I wasn't looking forward to it.

Let me back up a little bit and fill you in on why all this felt so deeply confronting. When I first moved to Austin, I found a church. But not just any church—a church that spoke to me on a deep level. It was different from any other church I had ever set foot in. In fact, it was so different I still sometimes have trouble calling it a church because it's not what you think. I experienced in this church a spiritual depth I never had before, and that experience was paired beautifully with an openness and expansiveness that I hadn't found even in most secular spaces. To put it bluntly, I found my home. I felt it the moment I walked through the door, and it was confirmed over and over to me as I became more and more a part of the community. The Church of Conscious Harmony (CCH) is where I discovered the Gurdjieff work and deepened my understanding of the Enneagram. I refined my meditation practice and for the first time became a part of a community focused solely on the work of becoming who we really are. I developed relationships and friendships that supported me and helped me grow. I blossomed in this space, with these people. I don't think I could possibly overstate how much I owe to this community. This is where I learned the true power of community. I had never experienced a community like this, and I was thrilled to find myself being weaved into the beautiful tapestry that was this church. And then there was a tear.

Three years into my time at CCH, the minister who started the church in his living room nearly thirty years prior retired. It wasn't a surprise, but I was caught off guard by how much the transition affected me and affected me negatively. It was a deeply painful transition, and I was trying my best to "hang in there." At the suggestions of several of my close friends in the community, I took a break. The timing was such that I ended up giving up church for Lent. It was a fruitful forty days, but even when I came back, things still felt too hard. So eventually I stopped going altogether. I had lots of excuses for why I wasn't around when friends reached out, and after several months, I had even convinced myself that it was time for me to move on. The problem was that every time I ran into someone from the community, I felt the same itch—or maybe it was a pull—and I found myself wanting to go back home. I wanted to go back to the church and community that had raised me in so many ways, but I felt like I couldn't. It had been too long, things were too different, I wasn't the same anymore. I repeated all of these reasons to myself over and over when I felt that pull, until eventually, it would slowly fade into the background.

But when I started fleshing out my ideas for this book, ideas around how to put the Enneagram to work in your life, having an intentional and Conscious Community to support your personal work was absolutely nonnegotiable. I knew when I signed the book contract that I was going to have to eventually deal with that pull I kept feeling. I couldn't write about the need for community, and how to do community well, while leaving all my baggage unattended.

Well, I'm finally writing this section of the book, so you can rest easy knowing that I am at the very least in the process of unpacking that baggage. And who knows, by the time you read this, these particular bags of mine could be completely empty! But before I dive into that process, I want to highlight more of what community offers us and why it's so deeply important that we have not just a community but many communities in order to support our personal and spiritual development.

WHAT COMMUNITY OFFERS

Community offers us some very special and meaningful things we can't get elsewhere—and we really need these things. Humans are social creatures. Evolutionarily speaking, we are not the strongest, fastest, or least vulnerable of the mammals, and while our sheer dominance of the planet is often linked to our extraordinary intellect, the truth is that our intellect would be useless if we weren't able to come together and cooperate with one another. As they say, there's strength in numbers.

Let's get real, though; we're a looong time away from when our ability to find and create community was keeping us safe from saber-toothed tigers and allowing us to hunt mammoths. In fact, the West has been dealing with the rise of individualism for the last several hundred years. We've evolved to a point where a person could plausibly live their entire adult life with little to no meaningful interaction with another human. Imagine a person who works from home, orders their groceries and food from the many apps available, and is estranged from their family. Someone could live their entire life without ever leaving their home—without ever speaking to another human! Even as I write these words, I can feel the heaviness of that kind of existence—and I'm sure you can too. (Especially because in the time since I first wrote those words, we have all been, at least somewhat, forced into that kind of existence because of COVID-19.) We feel this weight because, whether or not our mortal safety is at risk, we still have a deep desire for community. While community's value culturally is probably lower than it ever has been in the history of our species—simply because many people no longer need it in order to survive—we do, in fact, need it to thrive.

This thriving is because being in community feeds parts of our humanity that nothing else can. Community in its very nature provides us with safety and support, a greater sense of meaning and impact, and, maybe most importantly, just the right amount of friction needed to light and feed the fire of our personal and spiritual transformation. Exploring and understanding these essential elements of community can help inspire us to develop our own communities as well as help us understand when our community rubs us the wrong way if it's time to leave or if it's time to grow.

SAFETY

Humans are social creatures. We create communities everywhere, around pretty much everything. This is in large part because of the safety we feel when surrounded by known, like-minded people. Community can provide physical and psychological safety, both of which are necessary for our journey with the Enneagram.

It's easy to latch onto the idea of community providing physical safety when we think of cavepeople working together to take down a woolly mammoth or fend off a pack of prehistoric wolves (in my imagination, those wolves are much bigger and scarier than the wolves we have now), but physical safety might seem less important in today's modern technological world. It wouldn't be a stretch for me to assume that the majority of people reading this book don't fear for their physical lives when stepping outside of their homes on their own each day. The reality is, though, that we are capable of walking outside our front doors each day because of the social contract we've entered into with the larger communities known as our cities, states, and countries, and sadly, that social contract doesn't extend to all people. As a white person who is assumed to be cisgender and is able-bodied, I have very little trouble with the greater social contract that ensures my safety in my everyday life. Now, when I leave Austin and venture into the rest of the state of Texas or even farther into the conservative and more rural parts of Oklahoma, Arkansas, Missouri, and Kansas where my immediate and extended family live, I find I encounter a greater sense of fear for my physical safety. As a queer and nonbinary person, being outside of my community means I'm at a higher risk of physical harm. This risk goes up the farther you are away from our culture's implicit (and sometimes explicit) standard of being straight, white, cisgender, Christian, able-bodied, thin, and neurotypical.

What's fascinating about this phenomenon is that the level of engagement in community a person develops increases the further outside the standard they find themselves—and this is no coincidence. As we find ourselves at a greater risk of physical harm, we will be driven to find and/or create communities in order to protect ourselves. I realized I was queer while living in a small town in Arkansas, which, as you could imagine, was absolutely terrifying. I was reminded daily of my vulnerability and how quickly I could end up like Matthew Shepard, one of the most famous victims of homophobia at the time. The perception of a constant threat to my physical safety took its toll on both my mental and physical health. It was overwhelming, to say the least. Things started to shift, though, as I became a part of a community of other queer people who were living in this small town. We had monthly "Rainbow Dinners," where we could gather together with food and drink (there was always one food or drink item that was rainbow colored because of course there was) and share our lives with each other. We could vent about our fears of being who we were in such a hostile environment and our frustrations at the shallowness of the dating pool as well as share our excitement about our jobs and our dreams for the future. We even started a tradition (one that I still occasionally keep) of going out to the gay bars in the next town over on Saturday night and then showing up for church together Sunday morning. In short, we were able to simply live in the fullness of who we were without fear because we were surrounded by people who shared our experience. At those dinners and with each other, we had a reprieve from the fear that we carried with us nearly every moment of our lives, and because of this small break we found in our community, we all began to flourish. It's not an overstatement for me to say that this small community of queers saved my life.

Now, I wrote about physical safety first because it is required for psychological safety. If you are afraid for your physical well-being, your mind, heart, and body will all be focused on eliminating the threat of harm. You won't have any space or capacity to develop psychological safety. But when you feel physically safe, you have what is needed to show up in community in a more meaningful way. These two aspects of safety can feel hard to untangle because they so quickly fold back into one another. One way I like to conceptualize it which may be helpful is that if I am physically safe, I feel as though nothing bad is going to happen to me. I'm not going to be attacked. My physical body is safe. Then community provides psychological safety by creating the feeling of a safety net. In this case, even if something bad happens, I will be OK. I will be taken care of.

When I first moved to Austin, I worked at Starbucks. It was a wonderful job for what I needed at the time—the pay was decent, I didn't hate my coworkers, and I always had enough hours to pay my bills. Starbucks is also a very vocal supporter of their LGBTQIA employees. Combine that with the fact that I was working in a store that was in a very affluent neighborhood of Austin, and I felt very safe physically. I didn't love the work, though, and because of that, I didn't develop very deep relationships with my coworkers. After about five months, I started looking for another coffee shop to sling drinks at. This is when I found Stouthaus Coffee Pub, a coffee shop and bar in South Austin that had a great vibe and was run by awesome people. I felt like I was home from the first time I set foot in the shop. I convinced the owners to give me a job by telling them my favorite movie was *Mystery Men*, and I started the next week. As I worked at Stouthaus, I found myself being enveloped in an incredible community. Not only was I building deep and meaningful relationships with my coworkers, but several of the regulars became close friends. Even after only a few months, I knew that these were people I could rely on, people I could be open with, people I wanted to be in deep community with. I was experiencing psychological safety.

About a year after moving to Austin (about six months after starting my job at Stouthaus), my partner at the time and I broke up. It was a difficult and painful breakup. I was considering leaving Austin and moving back to Kansas to live with my sister and brother-in-law. I was in bad shape. My birthday was right around the corner, though, and my comrades at the coffee shop threw me a party. I will never forget that night. Tons of people showed up, my boss had baked me a cake, and all my coworkers had chipped in to buy me a really lovely gift. People had written in cards about how much they loved me and how glad they were that I was in their lives. I felt so deeply seen and cared for, and at a time when I was feeling so unsure of my direction and my place in life, this was profoundly impactful. I was able to work through and process not only the breakup but also the underlying questions of what I wanted my life to look like because I had the experience of being cared for when I needed it most. I had a community that supported me, and the safety that created allowed me to move forward and truly thrive.

It doesn't matter who you are—the world can be a very scary place, and life can be extremely hard. We gather in communities not just because we have a better chance of survival but because the support and safety we experience therein give us the space and capacity to live truly fulfilling lives.

MEANING AND IMPACT

Humans are wired to create meaning out of their surroundings. We have a strong desire to understand and make sense of the world around us, and we do that by assigning meaning to things. We also want to feel as though our presence matters. We want the fact that we exist here to have an impact on the world around us. In some sense, we want to feel as though our presence, our very existence, has meaning, and often we measure that by measuring the impact we have on those around us. So meaning and impact, two important elements of community, go hand in hand. They feed one another and are reciprocal in nature. Obviously, we all seek to make meaning of the world and have an impact on it in different ways, but no matter how we're seeking to make this meaning or have an impact, the two are intertwined. The more meaning we find in something, the more attention and energy we will bring to it, and the more impact we will have there. The more impact we have, often the more meaning we will assign to it. These two pieces are absolutely vital for developing a sense of purpose and direction in our lives that makes them feel worth living. Community provides us with a vehicle to create more of both meaning and impact.

When I was living in Arkansas, I had the great joy of working at another coffeehouse / record store called Pour Jon's (PJ's). Not only was this where I found my passion for exceptional coffee, but PJ's was also the central gathering place for all the different communities I found myself a part of during my time in Siloam Springs. It was owned and managed by my good buddy Chris. Chris and I became close because we both had our lives fall apart at basically the same time. When you're really going through it, there's nothing like having a good friend who's down in the muck with you. At one point, the coffee shop was having a really difficult time financially, and it was taking both a financial and emotional toll on my friend. Our community found a lot of value in Pour Jon's, not just because of the great coffee but because of the atmosphere Chris had worked so hard to create and maintain. This place had meaning to us, and we wanted to see both it and our friend really flourish. So in order to help, we organized a secret "cash mob," where we all showed up at the shop and basically threw a surprise party. We all bought drinks and records and were able to hand Chris a large chunk of cash.

Now, of course we were all individually still showing up on the daily buying our coffee and hanging out, but any one of us alone would not have been able to make the kind of impact that was available to us when we all came together as a community. All our efforts combined helped shift both the financial and emotional burden of running a small business in a small Arkansas town. The coolest part was that afterward, I felt more engaged and committed to the shop and to my friends, and others did too. When we all saw what kind of impact we could have as a community, we found even more meaning in the space where we spent our time.

As we engage more in our communities, they give us the opportunity to be a part of something bigger than ourselves, which is what so much of our personal and spiritual growth journeys are all about. As we align ourselves and our energies with our communities, not only does the community benefit from our presence, but we also benefit from the community by seeing our own efforts amplified.

FRICTION

Friction may be the most important piece that community offers us when we are engaged on our personal or spiritual journeys, and not surprisingly, it is also the piece that most often stands in our way. Any time two or more people are engaging, there is the opportunity for friction. No matter how compatible we may be, when we are in relationship with someone else, something will inevitably rub us the wrong way. We can even see this happen in our teacher/student relationships. The difference is that we often have very clear and explicit ways of dealing with the friction in these kinds of relationships, and when that can't happen, it's relatively easy to leave. Friction in our community is far more difficult to navigate. We lack the clear-cut ways of dealing with the friction, and there's much more at stake if we were to remove ourselves from these relationships—a classic double whammy.

Community, whether circumstantial or intentional, will create friction. No matter how much we try to avoid it, there's no way around it—and that's actually an extremely good thing. The friction and conflicts we have with other people show us ourselves, our boundaries, and where we are being invited into deeper growth and development. Without the little trip-ups and catches we experience when trying to relate to other people, we could easily become complacent and not move forward on our journey. We have to experience this uncomfortable friction if we want to grow. I love the analogy of a snake shedding its skin. Yes, there is some awareness that the skin is now too tight, no longer working, or unhelpful, but the skin doesn't just fall off. Snakes have to rub up against things in their environment to coax the old skin off. There is a certain amount of friction required in order for the snake to get to its new skin. Community can be one of the best places for us to find the friction we need to rub some of our old, crusty snakeskin off—as long as we know how to handle it, that is.

I don't know if I've ever experienced this as clearly as I have at the different churches I've attended over the course of my life. By virtue of my Enneagram type, I'm almost never the kind of person to just take something someone says as gospel until I've really worked it out for myself. And so I disagree—a lot—which, of course, brings a lot of friction. In the past, this has caused cracks and sometimes all-out breaks in my community. Most of the communities I found myself in didn't have the framework to effectively work through these kinds of frictions, and to be honest, I didn't have the capacity to stay long enough to give them the chance. I grew up in the church but left out of fury my senior year of high school because of the friction I was feeling between what the church was teaching and how things were being run. Basically, I deconstructed looong before it was cool. Of course, at seventeen, I couldn't have been expected to hold space for the friction I was feeling in my community, and it wouldn't have done any good because the community wasn't open to growing and changing in a way that would have made space for me either. This is extremely common in communities all over the world, not just churches. For both communities and the individuals who are in them to grow, both parties have to be capable and available to work with the friction that arises.

When I found CCH, though, I found a community that held space for disagreement and was willing to hold the friction people felt as they became more integral parts of the community. For instance, when I came back to CCH after my long break, I started attending a class on some of the fundamental principles of the church. I was excited to go and learn, but a few sessions in, some of the teachings started really rubbing me the wrong way. When I brought up my feelings to the minister, I was astounded at how well he listened to me and made space for my experience. We were able to have an open and honest conversation that brought us both to a deeper understanding of the topics of the class.

He was willing to learn and grow, and so was I, and because of that, we were both able to learn and grow in a way that would have been lost to us if I had either ignored the friction or used it as an excuse to just leave again.

It's important to note that you as an individual can grow and develop by staying in community and working through the friction you feel, and you can grow and develop just as much from removing yourself from the community if they are not willing to work through the friction with you. For the friction we feel in community to actually create space for us to grow and develop as a part of our community, both the individual and the community must be willing to grow and develop. Sometimes people see community as a whetstone for sharpening a knife; we're the knives getting sharper, and the community stays basically the same. The reality is, though, that the most transformative communities are the ones that are also actively undergoing the process of transformation and are using the friction of all their individual members to grow and develop. It's more like alchemy—everything is thrown together and somehow becomes more than the sum of its parts.

This is where we start to get into some dicey waters. Many of us are waking up to the ways that many of the communities we've been a part of, whether they're religious, business, or even our own families, have been less than healthy and enriching at their best and, at their worst, downright abusive. This acknowledgment of unhealthy communities is a clear shift in our collective consciousness that is very much needed. One unintended side effect, though, is that as we've become aware of these very real issues, we become hyper-vigilant and can start to perceive problems in places where what we're really experiencing is healthy friction. This is a difficult distinction to make because it's important to believe people who are coming forward and exposing abuse and to support those who have been taken advantage of, and as a community we need to be making a strong effort to develop our mental and emotional resilience to the point that we can withstand the normal levels of friction caused by being in community. With psychological language like trauma, abuse, narcissism, and gaslighting becoming commonplace in our vernacular, we must stress the importance of understanding their real meaning and how to know when they're showing up and when they're not.

We can't do any of this work well if we're not aware of how power and privilege play into these experiences. Because, inevitably, the person with the least amount of privilege will experience the highest amount of friction in community and is more likely to experience real trauma, gaslighting, abuse, and so on. So in some sense, my invitation into the friction of community is aimed at those of us who hold privilege, as we all are privileged in some areas of our lives and less privileged in others. It's also important to re-member that these issues are inherently messy. The lines are blurry, and there is rarely any sort of clear-cut answer. I can't stress enough how vital your personal practice and your rela-tionship with your teacher are as you move into these topics. The three legs of the stool are all equally important and act as a system of checks and balances for each other in order to help you see more clearly and respond more appropriately to the circumstances of your life.

Being able to differentiate between the normal and healthy (depending on how we respond to it) friction inherent in community and the abusive interactions we can have when our community is in disarray or downright dysfunctional and toxic is one of the most important skills we can develop on our journey of personal and/or spiritual growth. Again, there is no clear-cut checklist for this sort of thing, but as people familiar with the Enneagram, we can see how our types illuminate the subject for us. Whenever we are feeling friction that is directly related to our type, there's a good chance that this is something we can work with and work through. Each of the types might be more likely to throw in the towel over different kinds of friction. Yet if approached with care and compassion, these experiences could actually be transformative individually and collectively.

Type 1: Dear 1, it is so deeply important to remember that not everyone you are in community with is necessarily following the same rules as you, and even if they are, most of them are not as good at following them as you are. When you feel the friction of being in community with "rule breakers" or people who are less adept at acting with what you deem to be integrity, it's time to pause and ask yourself if you're holding yourself and everyone around you to an impossible standard. Maybe there is a more accepting way to move forward that would serve everyone, including you, better.

Type 2: Dear 2, as far as I know, no one in the world can actually read minds. You certainly come close with your anticipation of needs, but it can be helpful to remember that sometimes the best help you offer someone is no help at all. If you're caught in the friction of feeling underappreciated, it may be time to ask yourself if you've been doing more than what's yours to do and silently expecting too much of others in return. Paying close attention to what's yours to do and openly and honestly stating your own needs are transformative actions for you personally and for your community.

Type 3: Dear 3, being at the front of the line won't save you from feeling the difficult realities of being in community. Success in community means success for the community. What you think will make you successful personally may cause issues with the community as a whole. This is your invitation to look at what is truly valuable to you. Are you using your community as nothing more than an audience, or are you building relationships with these people? The friction you feel will often come in the form of failure. To be really in community with people, you have to allow them to see all of who you are, even the parts you want to keep hidden. By showing up honestly in your failures, instead of trying to repackage and rebrand them as successes, your community can show you that you're loved for who you are and not what you do.

Type 4: Dear 4, everyone needs community, even you. There are, in fact, a lot of people who share visions, values, and aspirations similar to yours. You may be surprised to find that there are even a lot of people who really do understand you. When you find yourself deep in the friction of feeling misunderstood or too impossibly different from those in your community, take time to ask yourself if you've given those around you a fair shake and if your need to feel special or unique is alienating you from the true sense of belonging that you deeply crave. The difference you feel, if you stick with your community, becomes a valuable asset for the community to thrive, and the community will, in turn, help you experience the depth of life more fully.

Type 5: Dear 5, you already know what I'm going to say—no person is an island. Your basic instinct is to isolate until you feel capable and "ready" to be in community, but the truth is that no one is ever really ready. When you feel the friction of "not knowing" how to be in community, take a moment to breathe and remember that the only wrong way to do community is to not show up. You already have everything you need to be capable and understand right here and now. By isolating yourself until you have it figured out, you rob your community of the opportunity to see just how you figured it all out. I coach many of my 5 clients on the value of "showing your work" or staying present to yourself and others while you work through your informational processes.

Type 6: Dear 6, no person and no community will ever be perfectly trustworthy. No community will ever provide you with the certainty you're hoping for. And honestly, that's a good thing, because if they did, you wouldn't be encouraged to grow. So when it feels like the community is conspiring against you, when you feel the friction of not knowing who to trust or when, pause and take a breath. This is a signal that you're not trusting yourself. Deep down you know the right move; you just have to quiet your mind long enough to hear it. This is how you grow amid the friction.

Type 7: Dear 7, this assignment is probably much harder for you than for the other types because you don't feel any friction, at least not consciously at first. Often, you're moving too fast to feel the tension and frustration that can often build in communities. Your job is to slow down and feel it. You aren't trapped in these relationships just because you might feel some friction. In fact, those things that are making you feel like you might be locked up are actually a signal that you have something to work on—something that could truly set you free. The true freedom you're looking for won't come by flitting off to the next thing but by learning to stay when things are hard and seeing them through to their end.

Type 8: Dear 8, it's likely that you avoid real and meaningful connection in community for fear of being betrayed. I'd like to tell you that you can finally relax and really participate in community and that you won't be betrayed, but the reality is, by your standards, you probably will be. But your growth doesn't depend on always being strong and never allowing yourself to be hurt; your growth depends on allowing yourself to be affected by both the good and the bad of what the world has to offer you. You will be betrayed, and it won't be the end of the world. You can learn to step more deeply into your own emotional experience and learn that the willingness to be vulnerable and be affected by life is your real strength.

Type 9: Dear 9, I know what you're thinking: "What friction?" Like our 7 friends, you're often immune to the overt and explicit experience of the friction that is common and normal in all communities. Your job, though, is not just to become aware of the friction that may be happening to other people; your job is to own up to and admit to the very real friction you feel inside yourself. Your job is to actually—*gasp*—create some friction of your own! You might fear that this kind of friction will mean you'll be cut off from the community you've grown to love, but the reality is that this friction means you're finally a whole and participating member of it. We all experience friction in community, and if you're willing, it will help you grow deeper in your connection with your community as well as deepen your own self-understanding.

CHAPTER 8

CIRCUMSTANTIAL AND INTENTIONAL

I'm writing this chapter in the first few weeks of the coronavirus outbreak in the United States. I am at my home in Austin with my wife and our two daughters. Danielle and I are trading off homeschooling duty throughout the day, but she's taking the lion's share of it while I try to finish this book and move my yoga therapy practice online. This time is incredibly scary. It seems as though, in a flash, we have lost all sense of safety, all illusions of certainty, and all sense of control. This chapter has been a struggle, not because it's a necessarily difficult topic to write about but because I feel like an exposed nerve, and everything about what I'm writing in this chapter is a reminder of how much pain I'm in. I hesitated to disclose all of this in the introduction of this chapter because things are so painfully uncertain. I have some fear that I would write this and, when the book comes out nearly a year later, all of this would have blown over. It would seem like a silly overreaction. But I have an even deeper fear that things will only get worse from here and it would seem as though I wasn't taking this seriously enough or, worse, this book will never actually see the light of day. After spending a lot of time with my emotions, I realized how important it is for me to give voice to these concerns. This entire crisis has really solidified how I think about community, especially in regard to the two pieces we're going to talk about in this chapter. It has also dramatically shifted my perspective in a few key areas that are quite literally changing the trajectory of this section of the book. I aspire to be someone who is always learning and willing to take direction from the universe (the divine, God, source, etc.) and change course at a moment's notice, and right here and right now I'm getting the opportunity to do that (and you get the opportunity to see it happen). So here goes.

We can categorize the communities we find ourselves a part of in two ways: circumstantial and intentional. It's important to make the distinction between these two types of community because they offer us different tools and support for our journey. Both types of community are equally important, but if we don't make the distinction, often we are not aware of how much community we actually have in our lives.

Circumstantial community happens purely out of circumstance: your family of origin, your job, your city or neighborhood. You don't have much or any control over who is in or out, and members of circumstantial communities are rarely drawn together by a strong moral or personal value. The "reason" that you have come together is often nothing other than the run-of-the-mill circumstances of your life. While your participation and active engagement in the community is optional, the fact that you belong there is much less so.

Intentional community is a community that is built with and for a purpose. Your engagement in this type of community is optional, and the amount of belonging you experience there is directly correlated to your level of engagement. These communities often originate in a "third space," meaning not at your home or at your job. Your intentional community could be focused on a hobby like photography or building model trains or can have a spiritual or religious focus like a church or meditation group. The main difference between a circumstantial and an intentional community is that in an intentional community, you are making an intentional decision to belong.

Now, there can clearly be a lot of overlap in these types of communities, and a community that is intentional for you may be circumstantial to someone else. The church or spiritual community your parents made a conscious decision to be a part of may have little to no meaning or value to you. You may have cultivated a very intentional community of friends, but when you enter into a new romantic relationship, that group will be a very circumstantial community for your new partner. What it all comes down to, really, is the following question: Did I choose to be a part of this community or was it just handed to me? The community has something to offer you, no matter what, but your answer to the question will affect not only how you participate in the community but also what you get out of it. It's important to note that both kinds of community are vital for our growth. Sometimes, though, even when we've made the distinction clear and we understand the different kinds of community we belong to, we have a tendency to put higher importance on our intentional communities and see our circumstantial communities as less important and deserving of less of our time and attention. This is especially true of our personal and spiritual growth circles. (And quite honestly, when outlining this chapter, I was prepared to place these categories of community into a hierarchy with intentional at the top, but like so many things in this moment in time, that idea was completely turned on its ear by COVID-19.) What I've come to realize through this ordeal is that when we talk about these two types of community, both are deeply valuable and necessary for our personal and spiritual development. Before I explain why this is true, we need to understand what each one of these types of community really is, what differentiates them, and what unique gifts they can give us.

INTENTIONAL COMMUNITY

As I just mentioned, in the course of our personal and spiritual development, we tend to place more focus on our intentional communities. The meditation group where we first had a taste of reality, the yoga studio that changed the course of our lives, the church where we found our spiritual home, and the disc golf team that has become like family all play a vital role in our journeys. They often take some time to find or build, and that building takes intention and effort. Because of this, they are usually the first (and sometimes the only) things we think about when we think about community.

Intentional communities ask something of us that our circumstantial communities don't. They come at a higher cost, and because of this, they offer unique value. First, we have to choose to be a part of them. We rarely stumble into these communities, and if we do, we don't stay unless we *choose* to. Choice is a powerful force in the human psyche. You don't have to have a doctorate in psychology to understand intuitively that when you choose something, you engage with it differently than when something is just handed to you or even forced upon you. The choice we make shifts how we engage with the community and also directly influences what the community can give us. As we engage more deeply, we experience a stronger sense of safety and meaning. Intentional communities also create the conditions for a higher likelihood of the friction we talked about in the previous chapter, which could seem like a downside, but alongside this increased level of friction, our intentional communities also provide a stronger commitment to working through it. In addition to the heightened level of safety, meaning, and friction, our intentional communities offer us focus and intimacy.

I have been in and out of different communities my whole life. There's something about my type-8 structure that has trouble really giving up the "loner" persona. I've hosted a few open mics in different cities, I've crashed my fair share of meetups, and I have even visited a number of churches and spiritual communities in my adult life. All of these places were intentional communities, but I didn't feel like they were really mine. It wasn't until I set foot in New Tribe Yoga—the studio in Siloam Springs, Arkansas, where I first found both yoga and Centering Prayer, years before I made my way to CCH—that I experienced the power of intentional community. At first, I was excited about the practice. I found something that was opening me up in a way

I had never experienced, and so I was there as often as I could be: power yoga four evenings a week, "Long, Slow, and Deep" every Tuesday night, and Morning Prayer yoga Monday through Friday at 7 a.m. My life shifted greatly because of my commitment to my newfound yoga and meditation practice, but I wouldn't have been able to stick with it if I wasn't *intentionally* engaging with the community that was also developing and cultivating this practice.

These communities provide us with the focus we need to keep ourselves on track, and without them, we'll be easily jostled off course by the demands of our daily lives. We may have particular bursts of growth or development on our own, but we are too distractible, and life demands so much from us. It is difficult to maintain course without the focus intentional communities provide. Yes, I'm sure it could be done, but you have to ask yourself: Why on earth would you want to make this harder than it needs to be? Whenever we have a goal or hope for growth, we are almost always best served by bringing it into an intentional community. This is because an intentional community, by definition, is made up of members who share a common intention. New Tribe Yoga's mission was to "become who we truly are, for the benefit of all," and that mission, or intention, was what we all had in common. It's what brought us together, it's what directed how we interacted, and even though I haven't practiced in that physical space for years now, that intention still influences how I relate to and engage with the friends I made there. An intentional community is where we go to be continually reoriented toward our goals because everyone (or most everyone) there shares the same goals or intentions. We're reminded of why we're doing what we're doing, and when our friends and comrades need reminding, we can be there to help.

Out of this community and the intentions and goals we share, we're invited into a new level of depth in how we relate to others. I've found many of my dearest and closest friends because of my time at New Tribe. Not only did we build deep and intimate friendships while we shared physical space together; we have also remained close even after moves and life transitions (which is something I had never experienced before). Intentional communities create a space for us to relate in a new way to those around us. Because intentional communities offer us a higher level of safety, we are able to develop more and deeper intimacy and connection with the other members of our community. In the midst of my first yoga teacher training, I was given the assignment of practicing at a couple of other studios in order to broaden my yoga horizons. At this time, there weren't that many options in Northwest Arkansas, so finding another studio was a tall order. My besties from New Tribe and I packed up and made the trek to Tulsa to try a Bikram studio there. The practice was underwhelming, but what made the whole event memorable was what happened when the class ended. We were stopped by a couple of different yogis who commented on our "vibe" as a group. They said it was obvious that we had practiced a lot together, that there was something palpable and refreshing in our corner of that hot and sweaty studio, and that they appreciated how connected we were. I've never forgotten that moment or that practice. I felt an immense amount of pride for my friends and teachers, and it was so incredibly validating to have someone see and voice what I felt when I was with them. We were connected not just because we did yoga together (because clearly everyone at the studio *also* did yoga together) but because we were in deep, intimate, and intentional community with each other.

CIRCUMSTANTIAL

As I admitted earlier, I used to believe that our intentional relationships and community do more for us than our circumstantial ones. But now, in the midst of extreme social distancing and the "shelter-in-place" order my city and many other cities and states are under, I am struck by the reality of what all of my circumstantial communities have offered me. And it's apparent that many other people are waking up to this same sobering fact.

For the first few days of isolation, I was surprised at how lonely I felt. I was with my partner and our kids, my close group of friends was connecting multiple times a day via text and video message, and I was even Zooming into my church's weekly services. I had assumed that *those* were my communities, and I was still intentionally connecting with them, but the extreme feelings of loneliness persisted. Of course, online interaction is quite different from in-person interaction when it comes to combating loneliness, but there was clearly something bigger going on for me. It took me a while to realize that I was a part of so many different communities that I was now cut off from. What I was missing, and what was driving these feelings of loneliness, were all things my circumstantial communities offered me that I couldn't get from my intentional communities.

After I stopped working at Stouthaus to focus on my work with the Enneagram, I became a regular customer there. It's still where I have most of my meetings, and it's where I've written the majority of this book. While I love their coffee and think it's the best in Austin, the real reason I go there is because of the community I am a part of there. The owners, James and Sandy, the revolving door of baristas, the tried-and-true regulars—all of these people know me in some way that feels hard to describe. They each hold parts of who I am, and I them. Even though our personal relationship may not be that deep or nuanced, there's an amazing amount of care that we all share for each other. This is a very circumstantial community, and I have next to no intentional contact with most of these people outside of Stouthaus's walls. When we do run into each other out in the world, though, it's like a tiny reunion, even if we just saw each other the day before.

We all know how difficult it can be to make time for friends and community in this day and age. We have to work hard to carve out time and attention in order to stay close to those we want to stay close to. But our circumstantial communities are different. If our intentional communities offered us focus and intimacy, our circumstantial communities offer us belonging and ease, which are equally valuable. They require very little of us and offer so much—and this is where so much of their magic resides. Our circumstantial communities are often where we first learn and have a sense of belonging untethered to our net worth, level of wit, sense of humor, values, or beliefs—we belong simply because we're there. *That*, my friends, is downright magical.

When I was nineteen, I was pursuing my career in music with an intense amount of passion. I was living in St. Louis,

Missouri, at the time and had booked a weekend gig at a coffee shop in Paducah, Kentucky. I had played at Etcetera Coffee for the first time months before on a summer tour and had made friends with a few of the baristas. This particular gig was just as much fun as the first, and the baristas and I had a blast hanging out after the show. The next morning, as I was headed back home, I was sideswiped by another driver, and my car was left undriveable. Luckily, no one was hurt, but I didn't know what to do. I had never been in a car accident before. I was hundreds of miles from home. Oh, and I was a musician, so I had *zero* money (I was so broke that I look back and wonder how I even survived). The only thing I could think to do was call one of the baristas and tell them what happened. He came and picked me up from the scene of the crash and took me back to the coffee shop. Word spread fast in the small West Kentucky town, and soon I was surrounded by all the people who had attended my shows and people I had never met. The entire community came out in full force to support me. The baristas at the shop hung out with me and kept me entertained, the owner of Etcetera let me stay overnight in the shop one night, and the next night a barista paid for me to get a hotel room. When Monday rolled around and I was able to get ahold of the insurance companies, they said I needed to fax them the police report. I clearly didn't have access to a fax machine, but the head barista found a wonderful older couple a few blocks away who did, and they welcomed me over. After being stranded in this small Kentucky town for three days, one of the baristas graciously offered to drive me back to St. Louis, since my car wouldn't be fixed for another week.

Now, recall that I had only met a few of these people once before, and most I was meeting for the first time while shipwrecked in their small town. All of the care and concern shown to me was not because of our deep or intimate relationship or our shared moral or political values; it was simply because I was there. Of course, this is an extreme example, but it's relevant nonetheless. Our circumstantial communities, while maybe not as tight-knit as our intentional ones, cast a wider net, so to speak. Their casual nature and unpretentious manner give us the sense that we can show up as ourselves, as our belonging isn't tied to our beliefs, values, or even aspirations (this is, of course, more difficult for some types than others, but we'll talk more about that later). This low-stakes approach to relating to people gives us the chance to, to use a musical concept, "jam" in our relationships—we can simply play without worrying about not knowing how the song will turn out. We can try things on that might seem too scary in our more intimate relationships. As an 8, I notoriously have trouble asking for and accepting help—and always have—but in the story I just shared with you, I was able to allow myself to be held by the kindness of complete strangers. I could show up fully in my weakness because the stakes were lower with these relationships. I was able to "try on" accepting help because of the sense of ease I felt in that small town.

Now, you don't have to have a car accident and get stranded in a small town in Kentucky to practice "jamming" in your relationships. We're given the opportunity to jam multiple times a day, and we don't even realize it! It's called small talk. In personal and spiritual development circles, I often hear people complaining about how much they hate small talk. Those who view themselves as more "spiritual" or "awakened" just don't want to chitchat about the weather. I fell into that line of thinking for quite some time. I just wanted people I could "go deep" with. As I've grown to be more aware of how I'm relating to people, though, I've realized that what seems so trivial and "surface level" is actually an incredible exercise in authentic relating and is the perfect place to "jam" with other people. Small talk is the essential language of our circumstantial communities. It creates a space where we can find mutual understanding and connection with a complete stranger, which is an incredible thing, even if we are only talking about the weather. It's in small talk that we are reassured of our common humanity. It should be noted as well that this isn't just an introvert versus extrovert thing. Yes, there are people who may enjoy small talk more or be more adept at it, but regardless of your skill or comfort level, small talk is still a valuable method of communication. Yes, I usually prefer deeper conversations, but small talk can turn into "big talk" very quickly if we show up to it fully.

Small talk is actually one of the big reasons I loved being a barista—I could have microinteractions with people many times a day. As I look back on all my time as a barista shooting the breeze with people across the counter, it's clear to me now that this willingness to small talk actually helped me not only develop a stronger sense of my own circumstantial communities but also discover the best places to focus my attention to build my intentional communities. This is quite possibly the most valuable thing that our circumstantial communities give us: fertile soil for growing the intentional communities as well as our ability to show up to them well. As

I've already mentioned, I grew a strong circumstantial community during my time as a barista at Stouthaus. In allowing myself to really show up for this kind of community, I also developed many of the relationships that make up my very intentional communities. I made small talk with several regulars from the other side of the bar, and pretty soon we were hanging out outside the shop. Now when Danielle and I have house parties and people ask how I got to know everyone, the majority of the stories all start at Stouthaus. If I hadn't been as willing and able to engage in my circumstantial community, I would have never found the key players in my intentional community.

GROWING OUR COMMUNITIES

There is only one way to truly build community, and that is to engage with it. In other words, reading this book won't give you a sense of community. You'll only get that by going out and *engaging* with the communities you're already a part of. But this isn't always easy. In fact, most of the time it's pretty hard. And to top it off, we most assuredly will, in nine different ways, make it harder than it needs to be. Each type will struggle with different aspects of engaging with their community, but there are two things that we all tend to do that get in our way. The first is that we often don't recognize the communities we're a part of. We certainly can't engage with something if we don't even know it's there. Then, once we can see it, we tend to relate to it only from our patterns. Our engagement is limited by our type, and it's rarely questioned. If we can work through these two issues, we'll be able to fully engage in community in a way that will enrich our personal and spiritual journeys.

It may be the PTA at your kids' school. It may be the D&D group you meet with each week. Maybe it's the people in your power yoga classes or your neighbors in your apartment complex. You're literally steeped in community—it's all around you!—even if you can't see it at first. Like I mentioned earlier, when I was first outlining this chapter, I thought my only communities were my close group of friends, my family, and my church. But as I've become more sensitive to the idea of community, I can see how I am deeply woven into the tapestry of so many communities. For the last six weeks, my family and I have been essentially shut-ins, cut off from our typical ways of relating to our community. While at first I was feeling deep loneliness, as I became more aware of my circumstantial community in my neighborhood, I began feeling more connected than I ever have. Just this afternoon, a neighbor dropped off baked goods from a local bakery "just because." Yesterday at the grocery store another neighbor, whom I had never spoken to before the quarantine, and I recognized each other—even through our face coverings—and had a great chat (from six feet apart). While this global crisis has been incredibly difficult, I am grateful for how it has shone a light on all the different ways I am interwoven into my community that I wasn't aware of. It's brought me into closer relationship with my neighbors. Even as I was feeling cut off from some of my communities, I was given the opportunity to grow my relationships in a community I rarely gave any thought to. Now that I'm aware of these different communities, I'm able to engage with them more fully.

Of course, as we engage more in our communities, we must be watchful for how our types will show up and want to dictate how we interact. Each of our types has habitual and patterned ways of relating to community that, while they may have served us at some point, are often no longer useful and certainly don't help us grow and develop. As we become more aware of our type's unconscious way of relating to community, we can engage in practices that help us relate more consciously to our communities. This new and more conscious way of relating to and engaging with our communities opens us up to experience the kind of community that is truly transformative in our personal and spiritual development.

CHAPTER 9
CONSCIOUS COMMUNITY

I had been teaching the Enneagram for a little over a year when I decided to take my show on the road and book myself a few little teaching tours. I've always loved traveling, and I was ecstatic at the thought of having an excuse to get back on the road. By the time my teaching schedule took me to Kansas City, I had several months of travel under my belt and had come to expect a certain predictable flow to the workshop. But this particular workshop would turn out to be rather unique. I set it up through some connections I had made in the Narrative Enneagram community, and I was thrilled to discover that my new internet friend, Nhiên Vương, had been combining Enneagram wisdom and contemplative practices in her community at Unity Temple on the Plaza for several years. When I arrived ready to teach my Embodied Enneagram workshop, I was greeted by what I can only describe as an extremely Conscious Community. Teaching there was an absolute blast and a very high honor.

Individually, it was clear that each of these people had a strong understanding of the Enneagram and were also engaged in their own contemplative practices, which is honestly a sight to see. But it was more than just having a handful of extraordinary individuals in a room together. They were clearly a cohesive unit. The container we created as a group and the space we were able to hold for each other felt so safe that what we were all able to share and create during our time together was much more impactful than your run-of-the-mill workshop—not only for the participants but for me as well. Normally at the halfway point of a day-long workshop, I am in need of some serious alone time. I often take my lunch break by myself, away from the participants, but this time I felt energized by being with these people. We all went to lunch together and talked and laughed. It was incredibly life-giving. I still consider this workshop one of the best I have ever taught and remember the experience of being with these people, this community, very fondly.

This isn't a coincidence. This isn't just a random happening. This experience was so life-giving for me as a teacher and as a spiritual seeker because of the Conscious Community these people had forged together. As we start to examine the ways our type structures habitually and unconsciously relate to others in our community and engage in the work to dismantle their unhelpful patterns, we inevitably find ourselves in Conscious Community, and the more people actively engaged in this work, the more transformative it will be not just for each person individually but also collectively.

WHAT IS A CONSCIOUS COMMUNITY?

All Conscious Communities are intentional communities, but not all intentional communities are Conscious Communities, just like all squares are rectangles but not all rectangles are squares. Where an intentional community may be built around a myriad of different goals or intentions, a Conscious Community is an intentional community whose members are actively engaged in the work of relating to each other and the world around them from a place other than their habitual and unconscious patterns, both on an individual and collective level. Individually, this means that each person is working with their type in relating to each other person both inside and outside the community. Collectively, this community is also engaged in looking at how they habitually see and respond to the world as a whole. This means developing a collective self-awareness around not just how type energy is playing into the culture of the group but how more insidious and unconscious issues of race, class, sexual orientation, gender identity, and ability dictate the groups dynamics. As you might imagine, this is an extremely tall order. Conscious Communities require a new level of personal and collective commitment because it is the combination of our personal intention and experience as well as the intention and experience of others in the group that makes a community "conscious." With this new and deepening level of commitment comes a new and deepening level of intimacy, which, similar to our intentional communities, creates more opportunities for meaning, impact, and of course, friction.

Creating and maintaining a Conscious Community is not easy. In fact, it may be the most difficult step of our personal

and spiritual development. When I first joined CCH, everything was wonderful! I loved the people, the space, and
the things we were learning together. But as I grew, I was
faced with more and more of my own personal and spiritual junk, and it wasn't pretty. I was also faced with some of
the community's junk. Even in this magical space with these
wonderful people, I started to experience the undercurrents
of racism, sexism, homophobia, and transphobia. These
weren't overt and outright experiences; they were much more
subtle and marked by an unwillingness to see the darker,
more shadowy underpinnings of the community's collective
unconscious. When I brought up the fact that we are an extremely racially homogenous church and asked what we were
doing to actively become more diverse, I was told the church
just does what it does, and the rest is up to spirit. While that
may seem like a perfectly fine answer, it clearly shows a
block (or what the Gurdjieff work would call a buffer) that
was preventing our community from moving forward and
actively engaging in racial justice. When I asked about why
the church, which is obviously LGBTQIA-affirming, hadn't
made an official statement on its website about it, the answer
was that we don't focus on or celebrate aspects of our personality (which is where sexuality and gender are lumped
into in the Gurdjieff work). Again, not a bad answer or approach on its face, but without the collective self-awareness
that churches are seen, as a default, by queer people as
dangerous and harmful places, the community was inad-
vertently cutting itself off from hundreds if not thousands
of people in our city who are actually hungry for the kind of
spirituality that CCH teaches and practices. In our personal
and spiritual work, we must be willing—both individually

and collectively—to question our actions and motivations in order to continue growing and developing. Eventually, I decided to leave CCH. I believe that was the right move at the time, but it became more and more clear that staying away was not going to ultimately serve my personal and spiritual development. When I finally came full circle back to CCH, I was hesitant to bring up the issues that caused me to leave, but as I began to share my concerns with the new minister, they were met with open ears and an open heart. Things began to shift, and not a moment too soon. As you may remember, shortly after the initial COVID-19 outbreak in the United States, there was a collective "waking up" to the realities of police brutality against Black and Brown bodies inspired by the murders of George Floyd, Breonna Taylor, and far too many others to count. This kind of communal consciousness work takes time, but it is so deeply worth it.

Conscious Communities require more commitment, more time, and more energy and often cause more frustration and pain. That's why so many people (like me) opt out and subsequently why so many people (again, like me) feel stunted or limited in their journeys and so many communities remain dysfunctional and toxic. When it comes to Conscious Communities, it can be difficult to justify the extremely high cost, but this is simply because we don't understand that the value is even higher.

WHAT DOES A CONSCIOUS COMMUNITY OFFER US?

On a very practical level, our Conscious Communities offer us a space to practice or try on new ways of being in the

world. As we attempt to live less from our habitual and unconscious type patterns, we need spaces that will hold us
with care and compassion as we fumble through our growth.
Not every community is capable of doing this, but each of us
will definitely fumble, so Conscious Communities play a very
important role in our growth. If I just left it at that, it should
still be enough to inspire you to become a part of a Conscious Community, but the focus would be too narrow—too
individual. Our true development doesn't end with us; it is
collective by its very nature. So much of Enneagram wisdom talks about our journey toward experiencing wholeness,
but our wholeness can never be fully experienced individually. In a culture that is hyperfocused on individuality, this
may come as a shock. In a lot of the self-help and personal
development communities, we hear that we are whole—as
in, we are not broken people. To this extent, I agree with
this assertion, but that is as far as I'm willing to go with an
individually focused idea of wholeness. Wholeness, in the
ultimate sense, is not merely about us as individuals but is
about what we can experience as we grow in community and
connection with one another—learning to hear other voices
and perspectives, learning to love all the infinite differences
there are between us while understanding that we are intricately connected. This is the kind of wholeness our Enneagram work is really inviting us into. We are finite beings and
will always have limitations to what we can see, experience,
and understand. That is exactly why we need community.
By being in community with another finite being who sees,
experiences, and understands things differently than we do,
we get to experience more. We can only experience our true
wholeness in community. This experience of true wholeness

starts in our Conscious Community. But to be honest, most of us have a lot more of the practical work around community that we need to do before we can experience this kind of wholeness, so let's dive into the more practical aspects of this kind of community.

The work of divesting from our type structure and becoming a more conscious being is inherently messy. It's messy because, just like with learning any new skill, we're trying to do something we don't have any experience with. On top of this, we have the added block of our personality seeing anything other than our patterns as inherently unsafe. To go against the pattern would be a mistake—and a mistake that our ego believes could prove fatal. It sounds like hyperbole, but if you've ever found yourself in the position of going against your personality pattern, you know that it can feel terrifying and unbearable. Maybe the trickiest thing about this whole process is that our ego keeps receipts, and we are afraid to step outside of our type structure because our past experiences with those behaviors were painful and possibly even dangerous.

During my time in Arkansas, I became fast friends with a guy who I'll call Paul. He was one of the first people I came out to, and he played a huge part in connecting me with the community I so desperately needed. We ended up becoming roommates because neither of us could afford to live on our own, even in our small town. Everything seemed to be going well until my life started to deteriorate. My finances and mental health both gave out almost completely, but I had been engaged in my personal yoga practice and was learning more about myself through the Enneagram and decided to try a new approach. Instead of continuing to push myself, handle everything on my own, and hide how I was struggling, I owned up to my situation and asked for help. I shared with Paul about how I was on the verge of being suicidal and how I was filing for bankruptcy, but instead of being met with the care and tenderness I had hoped for, I was met with anger, aggression, and cold-heartedness. I was shocked and devastated. I had assumed that if I was "doing the work" to not show up in my type, everything would end up rosy. But it didn't. In the months that followed, our friendship fell apart, I ended up moving out to live with my parents, and I withdrew almost completely from the rest of our group of friends.

It would be easy to see Paul as the bad guy here, but he wasn't. He was just a dude doing what he could when someone he trusted let him down. Like I mentioned earlier, we're often not good at the things we don't have experience with, and I certainly didn't have any experience in genuinely asking for emotional support. I didn't do it well. I expected too much of Paul and wasn't able to take enough responsibility for myself. I was so wrapped up in my struggles that I wasn't able to see how much they affected Paul, both emotionally and financially. Choosing not to react to my struggles the way I always had in the past also affected him. I was putting him in a position he didn't agree to and wasn't prepared for. I had assumed that I could just open my heart up and spill my guts, so to speak, and that he would magically be able to see and support me in exactly the ways I needed. Obviously, that was not what happened at all. In response, I shut down, and it was as if my 8ness came back stronger than before, which of course didn't make matters any better.

Our type structure is built around the idea that we have to avoid certain things—in my case, being vulnerable—in order to stay safe. As we start to confront that story, if we're not careful, we will relive our worst fears, like I did with Paul. For a long time, I was angry with Paul and felt very betrayed not only by him but by this new path I was on that seemed to promise a peaceful and enlightened existence if I just followed the steps. I've done enough work around this situation now to realize that, while I was very excited about my new journey and new path, I was still very immature and had a long way to go to understand how this work really played out in my day-to-day life. As we do this work, situations like what I experienced with Paul are inevitable. If those are our only experiences with stepping out of our patterned behavior, we won't stick with this work long enough to actually gain the skills we need to live into new behaviors. Essentially, we need a place to practice new skills and build resilience before we can successfully take those skills out into the wider world—and this is why we need a Conscious Community.

A Conscious Community is a place that can make space for the ways we fumble through our own personal growth, and we can make the same space for other people. It is our place to make these inevitable mistakes where the stakes are low and our deepest fears are less likely to be realized. This community has to be intentional because we have to make very overt agreements about how we will and won't react and respond to people when they show up in their messiness. This kind of community becomes like a practice studio for real-world experience. Slowly, through practice with this community, we build the resilience we need to take our new behaviors and ways of seeing and responding to the world into our day-to-day lives. More importantly, we begin to shift our motivation from one of avoiding negative outcomes to one geared toward experiencing the truth of who we are, regardless of how the world around us responds.

Again, if that were the only reason to develop and maintain a Conscious Community, it would be a good one, but there's more. A Conscious Community is greater than the sum of its parts. Yes, it's hard to understate the value of even a handful of individuals doing the work of "waking up," but a human's potential is deeply limited when they are only counted as an individual. A community of consciously engaged individuals not only provides benefits for each of its members but also has the potential to create a greater impact on the world around it than any of the individual members could have on their own.

The tagline or slogan for my first yoga studio was "Becoming who we truly are, for the benefit of the world." I have always found that so powerful and motivating. But when I first latched on to this idea, I will admit that I didn't have a very great understanding of what it meant. I thought that by doing my practice and "becoming a better person," the whole world would be better simply because I was in it, and now I was better. And I guess there is some truth to that—but it took time for me to realize that another layer of meaning lay beneath this inspiring phrase. As I grew and learned to accept more of the shadowy sides of myself, I became more accepting of the world around me. And through that acceptance, I could see the world more clearly. Because I could see more clearly, I could more clearly see the things that needed to be changed. I became involved in LGBTQIA advocacy, and I educated myself on issues of race and white privilege. I wanted the change I was experiencing internally to translate into greater change throughout the world, and I learned quickly that I couldn't do that alone. As we start to experience more and more of our collective wholeness through our Conscious Community, we get hungry for more! We not only want to see and understand the way the other members of our *community* see the world; we also want to see and understand how *everyone* sees the world. As we become more aware of our personal unconscious patterns and habits and seek to heal the harm they've caused, we have the space to become more aware of the larger societal and cultural undercurrents we're swept up in, correct them, and heal the harm they've caused as well. Individually, we can't have as much impact because we aren't talking about individual issues. We need a Conscious Community because these are community issues that we hope to shift. There is a Conscious Community at the heart of every great societal shift toward love, equality, and justice. These movements don't happen because one person became enlightened; these movements happen because a critical mass of people was willing to show up and do the work.

There are, of course, many degrees of a Conscious Community. It's not an all-or-nothing sort of situation. A community like this is always in a state of becoming, and there's always more room to grow and evolve. A community may be deeply engaged in and focused on the interpersonal work that is commonly associated with the Enneagram but struggle to develop a collective self-awareness. Conversely, a community may have a strong collective self-awareness and be focused on shifting larger cultural narratives while not actively engaging the work of dismantling the unconscious habits of its members individually. After I left CCH, my family and I started exploring some other communities. I was particularly excited about a Unitarian community in our city, as they had a strong focus on social justice work. As a nonbinary person, I felt safe and at home, as everyone who spoke at the pulpit shared their pronouns. The community had monthly social justice movie nights and was doing really incredible work in Austin and beyond. The trouble for me was that I didn't feel spiritually fed. It was like the messages they shared weren't for me in some way. Everyone we met there was incredibly kind, but there wasn't the same focus on a collective personal development, which was something I needed. This is an extremely common occurrence. If the focus of the community is too individual, the transformation that may be experienced ends up being stunted and ultimately self-serving for the community, whereas if the focus is too global without the balance of personal and internal work, the community will undermine its mission by unconsciously perpetuating the harmful relational patterns of its members. It could seem like this is an impossible balance to strike within a community. So the question begs to be asked, How do we create a community that is capable of all these things at the same time?

HOW DO WE MAKE ONE?

The idea of creating a Conscious Community probably feels pretty daunting right about now. The thought of somehow getting a bunch of people together who are all willing to both deep-dive into their own vulnerability, experiencing an intense level of intimacy together, *and* be available to unpack how covert and overt cultural messaging has shaped how they see and respond to the world seems preposterous. Honestly, because it is! When I underwent the process of becoming a member of CCH, I took classes and read books that acted as an initiation of sorts. They gave me the same foundation that everyone else in the community had. Maybe my favorite class, though, was the church history class, where Tim, the minister, shared the stories of how CCH came to be. It all started with a wish that he and his wife, Barbara, had to have a community of people committed to their spiritual practices and the Gurdjieff work. There were five couples that met in their living room, and over the course of nearly thirty years, the church grew to nearly three hundred members and now owns its own incredibly beautiful campus. The story always felt so magical to me—a real example of what a few consciously committed people can do. It has the romantic feel of someone setting out against the odds and doing the impossible, which of course we all love, but realistically, this probably isn't how most of us are going to go about creating our Conscious Communities.

When diving into this kind of work, it's fairly easy to assume that we're starting from square one and whatever it is that we need, we're going to have to build from scratch. But that is, first of all, a very individualized way of looking at this work (which, as we've been exploring here, is really communal), *and* it's incredibly impractical and inefficient. The reality is, *we aren't starting from scratch.* We're already a part of plenty of intentional communities that could very easily shift toward being Conscious Communities. Maybe you're a part of a community organizing group that's been doing advocacy work focused on serving the homeless in your area. Maybe you're a member at a yoga studio where the members are devoted to their personal practices and breaking free from their *samskaras* (loosely translated from Sanskrit as "patterns"). Maybe you're a part of a "mommy and me" playdate meetup group where you can let your kids play while commiserating with and confiding in other moms. All of these communities have the potential to be Conscious Communities if we're willing to show up less from our type patterns and invite others to do the same. Of course, you can always set off on your own and start from scratch in building your Conscious Community, but that process could probably fill a whole book on its own. For the sake of simplicity (and keeping this chapter to a reasonable length), I'm going to focus on sharing tips for transitioning existing intentional communities toward more conscious engagement.

GARDENING OVER MASONRY

In the book *Meditations on the Tarot: A Journey into Christian Hermeticism*, the anonymous author talks about the two approaches we can take to develop something new in our lives. We can be masons and construct whatever it is that we want through the force of our will, or we can be gardeners planting and tending to what we want to develop while surrendering to the will of life itself. In the work of either shifting an intentional community toward a more conscious one or developing a Conscious Community from scratch, it is important to remember that we must be gardeners, not masons.

We can't create a Conscious Community while unconsciously imposing our will on others. We can't force or coerce or manipulate others into doing this new thing we want them to do. As we seek to shift our current community toward more conscious engagement, all we can do is invite others into what we ourselves are already doing. Essentially, we're planting seeds. Some seeds may sprout and grow into something amazing, and others won't—and we don't have any say in which seeds do what. If we want to be successful, we need to surrender what we think we want that success to look like. When we become too attached to our ideas about how something should go, we become masons and start constructing something wholly out of our imagination—and our type structure—that will inevitably crumble (the masons/gardeners concept is found in the chapter on the tarot card known as the Tower, which depicts a large tower being struck by lightning and crumbling).

PLANTING SEEDS

Maybe my favorite lesson learned from my time at CCH is this: if they don't ask, you can't tell. When it comes to our newfound excitement around the Enneagram or building Conscious Communities, many people can become a little overzealous. If you've been in the Enneagram community for any length of time, I'm sure you've heard the term Ennea-evangelist, which is someone who is proselytizing and evangelizing for the Enneagram. It makes perfect sense that we would want to share this amazing new thing we've just learned about, but in our eagerness, we end up doing more "telling" than "showing." If we haven't done the work ourselves yet and experienced the tangible, meaningful, and sustainable change we're hoping for, why would anyone care about this new wonderful system we've found? When it comes to creating Conscious Communities, we don't plant seeds by shouting from the rooftops that we're building a Conscious Community. We plant seeds by quietly continuing to do our work. If we're doing our work, people notice and will want to know what's up. This is your opportunity to plant the seed. Again, if they don't ask, you can't tell. Also, as you begin to do your work, you will be more receptive and responsive to how other people around you are also doing their work. When you notice how someone in your life is shifting out of their predictable pattern, ask them about it! When we first engage in this kind of work, it can be easy to think that we're the only ones doing it and we have to recruit everyone to this new way of being in the world. The reality is that people have been engaging in this kind of work for millennia, and it's likely that there are people in your orbit who are already on the personal growth train and want to help you get on board too.

TENDING THE GARDEN

In gardening, we surrender to the flow of life, but we still have to show up to pull weeds, water, and shell out compost if we want the best results. As you see your Conscious Community start to take shape, there are some things that need to be in place in order to keep your garden growing as best it can. Just as you (hopefully) are reading this book and working to develop your own personal practice and a relationship with your teacher, other members of the community need to be doing the same. The ability for a community to raise its level of conscious engagement is dependent on its members staying committed to their practices and teachers. Without this focus on personal practice and the teacher/student relationship that supports them, a community's capacity to engage consciously, both with its members and with the wider world, will be deeply limited.

Just like any entity, our Conscious Community needs some form of leadership. Most communities are defined by who their leader is, but Conscious Communities are different, and because of this, the leadership looks very different. Often, once a teacher has gained a lot of students, they may want to bring them together to act more as a community. The problem with this leader-first approach, though, is that there is no check on the leader. We've seen the negative side of this type of leadership in many so-called spiritual communities that are more like cults. They operate like a pyramid—the closer you are to the top, the more power you have, and the leader or teacher always holds the most power. We see this happen in corporate settings, in families, and in a lot of religious contexts. Rarely is a community able to function in a healthy and mutually beneficial way when run like this. Often the members at the bottom of the pyramid are exploited and abused, while the members at the top are treated like royalty. This is not a recipe for personal or spiritual growth for anyone involved. Period. For a community to serve as a place for personal and/or spiritual transformation, the leaders have to work to remain as much on the same level as the other members as possible. This can be done by creating a system of checks and balances within the leadership of the community, but if the leadership is not actively involved with the other members of the community, then even the checks and balances won't be enough. Community is about contact. Community is where we come into true contact with people, with their best selves and their worst selves, and the way we show up from day to day also shifts and changes. If you aren't able to see the reality (i.e., the good, the bad, and the ugly) of the people in leadership and you aren't encouraged to show up as your full self (and with space made for all the good, bad, and ugly), then your "community" isn't allowing for the real contact we need in order to grow.

The key for leadership in any Conscious Community is that it's not about power or influence; it's about service. A Conscious Community is never hierarchical. It is always *communal* (hence the whole *community* thing). The difference between these two types of leadership is absolutely palpable within the community. When the leadership is focused on power, members will feel taken advantage of and manipulated. When the leadership is focused on service, all members of the community will feel empowered to show up as their whole selves and serve the community as well. This communal approach to the leadership and structure of the community is so important because in reality, we really are all on the same journey. Someone may have been doing the work for five years, and someone may have been doing it for fifty, but both still have something to teach and something to learn. Whether you decide to step into a leadership role or not, this approach and outlook on community makes our Conscious Communities so powerful because these communities can experience and leverage the collective wisdom and expertise of all its members for the betterment of the community and the entire world.

A NOTE TO THE TYPES
• •

Each of our types has specific blocks to this kind of community as well as very specific gifts. The more we understand these, the more easily we can work with our blocks, and the more clearly we can understand what Conscious Community has to offer us and what we offer in return.

Type 1: The fundamental belief of type 1 is that they must be "good" and "right," which of course looks different for each person who identifies as a type 1. This desire to be *and be seen as* good and right means that most 1s have trouble engaging with community until they've gotten themselves together. The problem is, this means they can put off being in community so long that they miss out on it altogether or that when they do engage, they tend to look down on other members who aren't living up to the 1s' high internal standards. This dynamic creates what I like to call "the high school group project effect," which is what happens when 1s believe that no one else in their group can do it as well as they can, so they end up doing it all themselves. This leaves 1s feeling resentful, irritated, and overworked and leaves the other members of the community disengaged, disheartened, and bored. As 1s develop their own personal practice and a relationship with their teacher, they can learn to relax and find their personal value and self-worth within themselves instead of in their striving for perfection. When this happens, they can start to let themselves, and everyone else, off the hook while still leveraging their idealism and integrity for the good of the community. Type 1s often provide a strong vision for their communities and can encourage and inspire all members of the community to strive for excellence. When 1s can relax the tense energy of their bodies and allow themselves to make mistakes, they can put the other members at ease and be more open to new and creative ways of reaching the vision they have for the community.

Type 2: On the surface, it would seem that 2s are perfectly equipped for community. Their orientation toward service and caring for others is a dream come true for any group of people they grace with their presence. The reality, though, is that 2s' apparently selfless giving and service is often motivated by the need to serve themselves. When 2s are operating unconsciously, they can weave themselves into the very fabric of the community, making themselves invaluable and indispensable, which will inevitably leave the poor 2 feeling overcommitted, overworked, and sorely undervalued. As 2s wake up to this fact, their dreaded unconscious move to the 8 energy can make them aggressive, combative, and destructive. This is obviously damaging for the 2 themselves, but it's also particularly harmful to the community they have made themselves so indispensable to. As 2s, with the support and guidance of their community, begin to turn their attention inward to their own experience and needs, they are able to open themselves to the reciprocity inherent in all healthy and conscious relationships. By slowing down and not being so quick to anticipate and meet unvoiced needs, 2s give their community the gifts of being able to practice asking for what they need and being more sensitive to the needs of others.

Of course, the community must be ready and willing to fill in the gap, or the 2s will surely fall back in, stunting their own personal growth and the growth of the community. If the community can make this shift, however, the 2s will be able to use their gifts of sensitivity and practicality to help the community see how they can be a greater force for love in the world.

Type 3: Community, and especially Conscious Community, is a difficult place for type 3. The tendency to treat their community as an audience is strong, and it can feel extremely challenging to show up honestly when there are so many people watching. It's much easier for 3s to either play the role of the star and position themselves as the poster-child for their community or play the chameleon and blend in so well that people never suspect they're playing a part and not showing up as their full and honest selves. Speed and efficiency, two of type 3s' deeply held values, are enemies of true, authentic relationships and therefore Conscious Community. It can be frustrating to 3s to realize that showing up as your true self in community is rarely pragmatic and almost never efficient, but this is where 3s are invited to grow. Slowing down and resisting the urge to either blend in or completely take charge will give the 3s space to relate to others from a deeper place. As 3s start to experience this deeper level of belonging and care for who they *truly* are, they offer their community a stronger sense of what is possible for the group as a whole. Of course, this can't be done without the community putting in work too. Our culture tends to make us uncomfortable when 3s decide to show up as their true selves, in their brokenness and failure. We'd rather use 3s as an example of what's possible when we just keep working (which

they certainly can be!), and seeing a 3 falter ruins that illusion. So just as the 3 has to work on showing up, the community must be actively creating a space where 3s know it's
OK to not have it all together. Type 3s have a natural gift for
tuning into the highest potential of people and communities,
and when they're grounded in Conscious Community, they
can use that gift to motivate and inspire their own communities to reach new heights.

Type 4: 4s' type structure creates the pattern of feeling
isolated and abandoned, even in a room full of people who
love and care about them, so community is really tricky. Their
fundamental belief that they don't belong goes hand in hand
with a fear that if they *do*, in fact, belong, then they would
be ordinary like the rest of us. The push/pull dynamic that
4s are prone to helps ensure that 4s feel like if they get too
close, things will fall apart, or if they stray too far away, they
will lose the sense of who they are without the context of a
community. All of this is compounded by the fact that, culturally speaking, unlike with type 3, we *really want* 4s to "get
healthy." Most communities don't hold a lot of space for the
emotional intensity and negative focus of type 4. So while they
are happy to hold space for the 4s' growth, there is rarely a
lot of grace or patience for 4s to show up in their type—and
without grace for how we show up in our types, there can't be
any meaningful, tangible, or sustainable growth. Communities need to be sensitive to the fact that if 4s are showing up
at all, there has been a lot of work to get to that place, and
4s need to understand that their feelings and intensity don't
always indicate the deeper truth and meaning that 4s think
they do. Because 4s focus on what's missing, they can have
a somewhat prophetic energy in communities, calling out

what could be but isn't yet. If communities can hold space for that energy and listen to 4s, they can experience immense growth. If 4s can stay grounded in a community long enough, they will start to experience the inherent truth not just in the darker, heavier emotions but in joy as well.

Type 5: It might seem like 5s and community are like oil and water. Type 5s' number-one defense mechanism is to isolate, so community offers a double whammy when it comes to their journey. It is almost guaranteed that 5s will experience difficulty in community that will make them want to isolate, but in isolating, they are cutting themselves off from the very growth and development they've been searching for. While it's vitally important for 5s to stay engaged in community, their community needs to understand that what engagement looks like for 5s is different from how others engage. That type 5s need to be and be seen as competent is most often what stands in their way when it comes to staying connected to community. They feel that if they don't have all the answers, they aren't bringing anything of value to the conversation, but this couldn't be further from the truth. When 5s can show up, even in their "unknowingness," they soon realize that the key to true understanding is experience. It should almost go without saying that a 5s insight and presence in a community is deeply valuable, but most communities miss out on what 5s have to offer because they often are moving too quickly or speaking too loudly to catch what 5s are bringing to the table. Just as the community slows down and becomes more sensitive to the 5's way of being, the 5 can be emboldened (with their connection to the 8 energy) and become a powerful guiding and grounding force for the community.

Type 6: A majority of 6s are driven to seek out community, and community often plays a very large role in their lives—but that doesn't necessarily mean they are doing it all that well. Type 6s are focused on building and developing community to help quell their fears of uncertainty and insecurity. They, like their 4 counterparts, can also get caught up in an unconscious push/pull dynamic, but it is more intellectual in nature than that of the 4s, being focused more on trustworthiness than emotions. Type 6s feel as though they must pull people close in order to see if they can be trusted, but then 6s compulsively test their trustworthiness, often pushing others away. Type 6s' work in community lies in relaxing their search for certainty and learning to trust their own authority—even while remaining in community. Certain members of the community may be especially susceptible to the 6s' desire to put people on a pedestal and then tear them down. It's important for all community members to remember that the goal of Conscious Community is to remain egalitarian and avoid idolizing/demonizing leadership. Type 6s also embody the "holy denying"* point on the Enneagram, which means they can often seem to stand in opposition of what the community wants. This isn't because they want to derail community interests, but because they want the community to be mindful of how they're moving forward. When the community can make space for the 6's objections, and the 6 can stay connected and grounded in the community, both can grow and develop more than they could have imagined on their own.

Type 7: The cliché is that 7s are always the life of the party, and to be honest, most of the 7s I know *actually do*

---

* See page 199 in appendix.

deeply enjoy organizing and planning fun get-togethers and experiences for their community. They have a gift for finding levity even in dark situations, which is, in fact, a very valuable gift in community. When 7s show up for community, though, their community often wants to pigeonhole them into only being the life of the party. For 7s to grow, they must be willing to explore who they are when things aren't bright and sunny. They have to learn how to fully experience the discomfort, pain, and suffering inherent in personal and spiritual development, and a 7 most certainly cannot do that without their community's support. The struggle for so many 7s is that their community doesn't want them to grow. I mean, really, who wants to watch your "good times" buddy start contemplating their own mortality? Type 7s have a lot of hard work in front of them when they start this journey, and it's imperative that their community creates enough space for them to move forward in their growth without the added pain and discomfort of feeling disconnected and unwanted by their community. Both 7s and their community benefit greatly when this happens. Type 7s find space and encouragement to engage in their Holy Work,* and the community can learn to hold both the painful and joyful together because of the 7s' example.

Type 8: There are two types of people in this world: the strong and the weak—at least, according to 8s. This pervasive way of conceptualizing the world puts 8s in an interesting position when it comes to community. Type 8s often fall into the role of guard or protector when relating to others. They can do this in a number of ways, from a position

---

* See page 218 in appendix.

of head leadership to quietly working on the sidelines. But the more they do it, the more 8s disconnect themselves from their community. In order to protect or lead, 8s feel they have to separate themselves from their community, but instead of making themselves better leaders or stronger protectors, this impulse hinders their ability to be either. Type 8s have a particularly difficult time with egalitarian relationships, as true intimacy requires vulnerability and is a direct threat to their type structure. It can be especially difficult for 8s to move out of this protector role in community, and one main factor is that many in the community *like feeling protected*. Often, when 8s attempt to step out of their protector or leader role, they're met with anger and disappointment, leaving the 8s feeling confused, taken advantage of, and betrayed. For 8s to be willing to step into true, intimate relationship in Conscious Community, the community must be willing to take their shift standing guard and give the 8s a break. When 8s can allow themselves to truly connect with their community, their innate strength, their deep understanding of justice, and their often hidden sensitivity to the most vulnerable among us act as a guiding light for everyone involved.

Type 9: 9s can sometimes get the reputation of being the model community citizen. They seek peace and harmony and are often natural leaders because of their ability to hear all sides of an argument. The truth is that 9s have just as much work to do as the rest of us. Gifted mediators when the conflict doesn't involve them, 9s have an extreme aversion to engaging in their own conflicts and are especially sensitive to the friction inherent in community. While most members of the community love having 9s around for their gentle and welcoming presence, this can often come at a high cost for the 9s themselves. Their tendency to numb out and ignore issues leads to a buildup of unacknowledged resentment and anger, which will eventually erupt. Type 9s must learn how to engage with these small minor frictions regularly in order to avoid such a destructive explosion later on. The community can help and support 9s by creating easy and open communication about differences and difficulties. Type 9s fear that any form of conflict is a threat to their safety and sense of connection to those they love. By making it clear that 9s are welcome and belong even when they're angry, the community can create the space necessary for 9s to fully engage with their inner work. As 9s embark on this journey, they become a truly valuable member of their community, creating a real sense of peace and harmony by helping everyone play their part.

CONCLUSION
BALANCING THE STOOL

I've found that understanding the system of the Enneagram isn't half as important as knowing how to do the work it's asking of us. Don't get me wrong, I love the Enneagram and think it's an incredibly powerful tool, but just like any other tool, it can only be as powerful as it is useful—and it's only useful if we know how to *use* it. Imagine having the world's most powerful computer at your fingertips, capable of taking a rocket ship to the moon or creating the next massive summer blockbuster or connecting people from all over the world and giving them access to education. And then imagine only using that computer for watching kitten videos on YouTube or getting into arguments with people on Facebook. Seems pretty silly, huh? But that's exactly what we're doing when we learn the Enneagram and only use it to laugh at memes or, even worse, as an excuse or justification for our less savory behavior. Sadly, those become our only options if we don't start to develop the three legs of our personal development stool. So let's see if we can put all these things together.

WHERE TO START

· ·

I wrote this book to help those who were interested get the most out of this incredibly powerful tool, and I know how overwhelming this approach can seem. I can't imagine someone reading through this book and then committing overnight to a practice, finding a teacher, and developing a community—it's just not possible. But what is possible is starting where you are and steadily working to develop each leg of your stool little by little over time. People often ask which leg of their stool they should work on first when they're getting into this work, and my answer is always that it depends. The first step isn't actually jumping directly into the work of practice, lineage, or community; it's becoming aware of where you're at with each of these. Awareness is key. As I mentioned in the "Circumstantial and Intentional" chapter, we often don't have a great awareness of how much community we're already in, and the same goes for our practice and lineage. We need to get curious about how we're already participating in each of these legs of our stool and how they're affecting our lives. This is essentially what I do with my clients during our initial session. I ask questions about their lives, their routines, their friends, and their relationships. I want to get as clear a picture of where they are as I possibly can, and then we'll know where and how to start working. Just like we need to have an understanding of our type before we can work with the Enneagram—in other words, we need to know where we're starting—we also need to have a solid grasp of how the aspects of practice, lineage, and community are already at play in our lives.

As an 8, I've always had a tendency to dive into the most difficult work first. So I would have, in the past, looked at what leg of my stool was the least developed and dive right into working on that. What I've found through that approach, though, is that it tends to make things harder than they need to be. As I've shifted my personal work to have a more gentle approach, and worked with many clients, I've found it's often more helpful and more sustainable to become more aware of which leg is strongest and spend time working with it in order to gain confidence and help us move into what may be the more difficult work for us with more ease and comfort. The beautiful and somewhat unexpected thing that happens when we engage this approach is that as we seek to go deeper into the leg of our stool that we are most comfortable with, most interested in, or most adept at, we will *need* to develop the other legs to keep moving forward.

Because I started my personal growth journey in a yoga studio, practice came easy for me. I had a daily movement and meditation practice that served me very well for years. As I started yoga therapy school, I had a really strong desire to deepen my practice, and what I found very quickly was that the only way for me to do that was to get a teacher. So that's what I did. I wasn't seeking a teacher for all the intrinsic value having this kind of relationship offers (or to strengthen the lineage leg of my stool)—I did it because I wanted my practice to improve and deepen. And it did! As my relationship with my teacher grew, though, I soon found myself wanting to focus on it for its own sake. Eventually, I realized that for both my practice and my relationship with my teacher and lineage to continue to develop, I needed a stronger sense of community, and so that's where my focus went next. But to say that this is the only place to start or that this is the one way to develop your stool would be foolish. I know many people who have an incredibly strong sense of community but next to no daily practice to speak of. Telling them they need to get a practice just doesn't work, but explaining how developing a practice will improve how they engage with their community is often exactly what they need to hear.

When we work on one aspect of our stool, it becomes easier to work on all the others. Now, it may not always be easy, but it will be *easier*. The stronger our sense of community is, the easier it will be to move into a relationship with a teacher and a lineage; the stronger our personal practice is, the better we will show up in community; and the deeper our relationship with our teacher, the more effective our practice will be. That's because while we can conceptualize all of the legs of our stool as something different, the reality is that it's all the same stool. I'm reminded of the saying, "At high tide, all ships rise." Everyone will start in a different place, which means everyone will have a different approach, and that's exactly how it should be.

CHECKS AND BALANCES

Of course, some people may read this and think, then, that it doesn't matter what leg you work on ever and will just continue to keep their focus on what feels easiest or comes most naturally. The problem with this approach long term, though, is that our stool will never be balanced. And just like all ships rise at high tide, all ships will come down at low tide. If one of the legs of our stool remains undeveloped, it will hinder our overall growth. We'll be stuck. Even worse, if only one leg is getting our attention and energy, it will undoubtedly stop supporting our growth and development and simply become another place where our type's patterns can run amok. We need to bring Conscious Attention and effort to developing and incorporating all three elements into our daily lives because they each act as checks and balances for the others.

Our practice is solely focused on our own individual and personal experiences. It really only involves you. And the impact of this practice is primarily focused on you. In so many ways, our practice is where we can really focus in on our growth and development. This is where we gain new skills and allow ourselves the opportunity to experiment with different ways of seeing and responding to the world. Without the outside oversight of a teacher and lineage, though, our practice can quickly and easily turn into something that reinforces our patterns instead of loosening them. We need a teacher to help us notice our blind spots and gently guide us toward the aspects of our growth that are most necessary at any given time. Without a lineage, we won't have the structure or scaffolding to give us the direction and purpose we need in order to stay committed to our practices long enough to see them become fruitful. If we focus solely on our practice and don't develop our sense and experience of community, we won't have any idea if our practice is actually working for us or if it's helpful for anyone besides us. The good work we've committed to in our practice will become stunted without the greater impact and meaning that we find in our communities.

Our lineage helps us connect to something bigger and deeper and also gives us a set of parameters to operate within. It's hard to overstate the value of feeling a true sense of tradition that both grounds you and inspires you—and this is what we find in our lineage. Our teachers, more specifically, bring us into relationship. This relationship, though, is hierarchical—the teacher is teaching, and we are learning. We are coming to the teacher for help and support, so there is an inherent power imbalance. Soon this kind of relationship could easily become abusive and manipulative if not checked by the more balanced approach to relationship we find in our community. Even when we've found and committed ourselves to the best possible lineage for us, it's hard to walk the road alone. Our community offers the support and spirit we need to keep walking the walk. If we aren't also focused on our practice, our student/teacher relationship will just be another place we play out and reinforce our patterns, and the experience of our lineage can quickly become dogmatic and shortsighted.

When we engage in and develop all of our different communities, we find safety, belonging, and a deeper sense of meaning for our personal work. Community is focused on relationship, but for the first time, the relationships are egalitarian. This is where we are connecting in a truly heart-to-heart way with other people. But if we aren't invested in our personal practice, our ability to connect to the people in our community in this way will be greatly limited. If we haven't developed a strong relationship with a teacher and lineage, we won't be able to access the help, support, and direction we need in order to continue growing. A community that doesn't have a sense of lineage and whose members aren't engaged in practice won't be able to do the work of unraveling the negative relating patterns happening inside the community and certainly won't be able to be a community that has a greater effect changing the unhelpful sociopolitical patterns of the wider world.

It's important to know where you're starting from, but it's also important to make sure you don't stay there. All three legs of your stool are necessary to continue growing and developing while using the Enneagram (or any other personal or spiritual development tool, for that matter). Growth happens little by little over time. Sometimes it may feel like nothing is happening at all, and then all of a sudden you look back and realize your life is completely different (and better!) than it was one or five or ten years ago. Being mindful of how you're engaging with your own practice, lineage, and community and being willing to adjust and change as necessary will keep you on your path and prepare you for what you find along the way.

THE KEY INGREDIENT

As we engage in this work (and believe me, it's work!), the way we do it matters. If we're only following these steps out of some sense of duty or obligation, we won't experience the tangible, meaningful, and sustainable growth that's possible for us. Maurice Nicoll writes the following in his *Psychological Commentaries of the Work of Gurdjieff and Ouspensky*:

> The work can only be done in the spirit of its own beauty and light, in the spirit of its true message and significance. Life on earth is nothing but a

field for working on oneself, so that one can return from whence one came. . . . For to work in
a negative way is useless. *It is only through some
kind of delight, some feeling of joy or pleasure
or some genuine affection or desire, that a person
can work and bring about any change of being
in [themselves].* Fear, for example, will not act in
this way. A person may have some knowledge of
truth, but unless [they value] it, unless [they feel]
some delight in it, it cannot affect [them]. It cannot act on [them], for a [person] unites with truth
only through [their] love, as it were, and in this
way [their] being is changed.*

In other words, we have to find joy in this work—and if
we aren't, we need to step back and reexamine what we're
doing and why. This, of course, doesn't mean that everything
we do in this work will necessarily be fun or enjoyable, but
what Maurice Nicoll is pointing out to us is that it's our genuine joy, desire, and passion for this work and what it offers
us that creates the real change.

This was absolutely revolutionary in my personal journey.
As I've mentioned, as a type 8, I tend to make things harder
than they need to be. I have some underlying notion that if it's
not hard, it's not real. If it doesn't hurt, it won't mean anything.
This is a narrative that I internalized throughout my religious
upbringing to an overwhelming extent. I was taught that I
needed to pick up my cross, deny myself, grit my teeth, and just

---

* Maurice Nicoll, *Psychological Commentaries of the Work of Gurdjieff
and Ouspensky* (Boston: Weiser Books, 1996), 10. Emphasis and gender-
neutral pronouns mine.

bear it if I wanted to grow and change because—according to some—that's just what Jesus did. The more I did this, though, the worse I felt and the less real growth I experienced. When I started in the Gurdjieff work at CCH, this idea of mine was turned on its ear. Suddenly, I was surrounded by people who were not just happy but truly *joyful*, even as they went through extremely difficult life challenges. Being not only allowed but strongly encouraged to find joy in the work I was doing changed everything about how I worked on myself. It wasn't until I embraced this approach that I could really allow myself to experience my more gentle and vulnerable sides in a way that didn't feel like taking bitter cough medicine. When I lose sight of the joy of this work, it is a surefire warning to me that I'm back to operating in my type structure. And the same is true in some way or another for all nine types.

Now, this certainly doesn't mean that we are to adopt some "good vibes only" approach to our personal work—quite the contrary. I see the "good vibes only" or "no bad days" approach to personal growth to be nothing more than a reactionary second force to the "grit your teeth and bear it" approach. In other words, it's simply the other side of the same coin. Because the truth is, we most certainly will experience bad days and bad vibes on our personal journeys. To try to avoid them only results in spiritual bypassing. But that doesn't mean that those times on our path are joyless. They may be difficult and even downright awful, but we can meet them in a way that says "yes" and with an attitude of hope and joy for what we may learn and experience through them. These hard times and rough patches of our journey are some of the most fundamental "yes, and" spaces of our work. "*Yes*, this really sucks, *and* I know I'm learning and growing through it."

Joy is the secret ingredient in making all our personal and spiritual work create the change we want to see in our lives and in the world.

JUST THE BEGINNING
• •

Well, friends, we've done it. This is the end of the book. As I sit on Stouthaus's freshly reopened (but still socially distanced) patio, I'm really in awe of what a journey writing this book has been. What I've shared with you here in the pages of this book has all been excavated from my life, and I share it not as just some theory that looks nice on paper but as a tried-and-true user manual for the incredible tool that is the Enneagram. Yes, I have shared from the particularities of my life. I've done so not because I think that my experiences are universal (I know they're not) but because I hope that by saying something specific and particular, we can find a deeper meaning and truth. Because that's what I really want: for everything in this book to be something you can put into action. My greatest wish for this book is that it helps clear a path for anyone interested in using the Enneagram for personal or spiritual development—that it makes putting the insight the Enneagram offers to work easier and more accessible for anyone who reads it. And maybe more importantly, my deepest wish for *you*—yes, you reading this—is that this isn't the end of just another book you've read but that it's the start of an exciting and life-changing new chapter in your journey with the Enneagram.

ACKNOWLEDGMENTS

An enormous thank you to Lisa Kloskin and the entire book team at Broadleaf Books. I still can't believe you all wanted me to write a book enough to make it happen. Lisa, your guidance and influence were absolutely vital to not only making this project happen but making it a success. You've made me a better writer and a better person.

Matthias Roberts, literally none of this would be happening if it weren't for you. From introducing me to the Enneagram, to elevating my work with your platform, to connecting me with Lisa, not to mention being an incredible friend, confidant, and cheerleader since our time in Arkansas, I am so grateful you are in my life. I can't wait until we can celebrate in person with lots and lots of queso. (Also, *Look at us! We're authors now!*)

Kimberly Culbertson, your friendship and writing expertise have supported me so much over the course of writing this book. I might have just imploded if you weren't there encouraging and guiding me through this process. I'm so glad that I can always count on you to be there to celebrate with me, show me where I could use a little more joy in my life, and still create space for the harder conversations. Your friendship is such an immense gift in my life.

Amanda Green, there aren't really words for me to express how grateful I am for your influence in my life. You have taught me so much about what it means to be engaged in this work and have set an example that I hope to live up to. I feel incredibly blessed to have you as my teacher.

Dad, Teresa, Mom, Rulon, Sarah, Corey, Jon, and Airika, thank you for being such a supportive and loving family. It seems as though my life is always changing directions with abandon, but your love and support have never wavered, and for that I am deeply grateful.

James, Sandy, and the whole Stouthaus crew, thank you for keeping me caffeinated and motivated throughout the process of writing this book, for creating such an inviting environment to write in, and for having such a huge impact on my life and spiritual journey. You taught me what it means to lead by example and to take responsibility for myself in a way that would inspire and support others. I wouldn't be where I am today without you, and I would most certainly be a lot sleepier.

The Dream Team, the Knit Wits, the New Tribe Yoga gang, the Pour Jon's fam, Eden Limited's "Best Crew Ever," and the rest of my Siloam family, I wouldn't have survived those years in Arkansas if it weren't for you. You picked me up, dusted me off, and told me I could make something of myself. You were loving, encouraging, and kind but never shied away from telling me when I was being a dumbass. My spiritual journey started because of you, and this work took root in my life because of the love, guidance, and support you offered me at every turn. I hope I'm making you all proud.

To my family at the Church of Conscious Harmony, again I feel at a loss for words to describe what you all mean to me. I have been deeply changed by my time with you and know that I will continue to be inspired to grow and Work for many years to come.

Lesley, Rick, and all of the Austin Enneagram community, thank you for creating a space to engage with this work in earnest. I'm grateful to have such a deep well of wisdom and experience in this community. I learn so much from you all and am lucky to call you all friends.

Terry, Rene, Peter, Helen, Marion, and everyone at the Narrative Enneagram, thank you for being such incredible teachers and incredible humans. Thank you for believing in me and supporting me over these last few years. I hope this work makes you proud.

Saving the best for last, Danielle, you were the one who first suggested I should teach the Enneagram, and I don't think either of us had any idea it would lead to all this. Thank you for loving and supporting me through this grueling process of not only writing a book but building this career. I know it hasn't been easy for either of us, but I feel so lucky that you're in my life. I am deeply in love with you, Juniper, and Farren, and I'm so excited about the life we get to build together. My deepest prayers were answered the moment we met, and I am so thrilled to have such an incredible partner not only in life but in this work as well. You have my heart forever.

APPENDIX

HISTORY

• •

When discussing the Enneagram as we know it, having a clear picture of its history gives us the context for how we can use it well today. The Enneagram of personality is often touted as an "ancient personality typing system." While it's easy to make this jump, it's vitally important to clarify that while the symbol of the Enneagram has been traced back to Pythagoras, the personality typology is still in its infancy.

Our Western understanding of the Enneagram is rooted in the work of a man named George Ivanovich Gurdjieff. Gurdjieff discovered the Enneagram in his travels through the Middle East and saw it as the perfect map for how energy manifested in the universe. He saw in it the three laws that hold the cosmos together: the law of one, represented by the circle, shows the inherent unity in all things; the law of three, represented by the triangle, shows the way all progress must overcome polarity; and the law of seven, represented by the hexad, shows the process all things must undergo to become fully developed. The Enneagram as a symbol became central to the process of human development that Gurdjieff taught. It's important to note, though, that Gurdjieff never taught personality typing. The closest he came was talking about what he called "Chief Feature," or what could be considered the crux of our patterned behaviors. Several decades later, those who would use the Enneagram as a personality tool aligned the idea of "Chief Feature" with our passion and fixation, or Habit of Attention and Habit of Emotion.

It wasn't until Oscar Ichazo, a Bolivian-born student of Gurdjieff and founder of the Arica School, made the jump from the points of the Enneagram being simply steps in a process to being descriptive of a person's personality patterns that the Enneagram of personality was born. It was what could best be described as a rough outline, and while it was obviously promising, Ichazo was also preoccupied with several other ways that the Enneagram could be used, which he called Enneagons. One of his students, Claudio Naranjo, then ran with the Enneagram of personality and further developed the rough outline Ichazo had taught into what we know today. Naranjo was a psychologist and psychiatrist born in Chile who studied under Ichazo and many others in his incessant search for the truth of humanity's reason for existing.

In the early 1970s, Naranjo began interviewing his clients and students and combined the framework Ichazo had developed with modern psychology. Through the course of fleshing out the Enneagram of personality, he also founded his own school of personal development that he named SAT, or Seekers After Truth, as an homage to Gurdjieff's original group. Naranjo partnered with another psychologist by the name of Kathleen Speeth to further develop the system through interviews of students and clients. Soon, though, the pair parted ways, as Kathleen felt the need for this system to be shared with the world. Early on, Naranjo was adamantly opposed to sharing such delicate information with large audiences. Up until this point, Naranjo had only taught in small groups, even after bringing it to the United States in the early seventies. He taught only to closed groups of spiritual seekers. Speeth, though, began teaching publicly, against Naranjo's wishes.

In most histories of the Enneagram of personality, the lineage goes something like this: Gurdjieff, Ichazo, Naranjo, [insert modern teacher]. While it's true that these men are the ones who made the initial leaps in developing this system, the Enneagram of personality wouldn't be on anyone's radar if it weren't for two women, Kathleen Speeth and Helen Palmer. In addition to being Naranjo's teaching partner, Kathleen Speeth was an accomplished clinical psychologist and student of Gurdjieff's Fourth Way. She was instrumental in the development of the Enneagram of passions and fixations and, after parting ways with Naranjo, was the first to teach public classes on this powerful system. If it weren't for Speeth, the Enneagram would have remained an obscure and esoteric tool used only in new-age retreat centers and some strands of the Christian church. Speeth's bravery and belief that this kind of transformational wisdom shouldn't be left solely in the hands of the initiated opened the doors for hundreds of thousands of people to learn about themselves through the Enneagram. One notable student of Speeth's was Helen Palmer.

Helen Palmer was a teacher of intuition and psychic reader living in Berkeley, California. She was drawn to

Speeth's public classes and found the Enneagram to describe not only personality but also nine different ways that people can access their intuition. After much study, Palmer began teaching her own classes and was soon approached by Harper Collins to publish a book on the Enneagram. *The Enneagram: Understanding Yourself and the Others in Your Life* by Helen Palmer was the first internationally published book on the Enneagram, and it opened the doors for millions of people to have access to the Enneagram's unique take on personal development. It also opened the doors for a considerable amount of pushback. When Oscar Ichazo got word that what he believed to be "his" Enneagram had been shared in book form without his permission, he took Palmer to court for copyright infringement. Luckily for us, and especially for me as I write this book, Helen won the case, opening the doors for the Enneagram of personality to be spread widely both through teaching and in print. Since *Arica Institute, Inc. v. Palmer*, thousands of books have been written on the Enneagram in hundreds of languages.

Thanks to the tireless work of teachers like Palmer and Speeth, not only have more people been able to grow and develop using the Enneagram as a tool; the Enneagram community has been able to learn more about the nuances of type and fixations as well as what true transformation can look like. Without these women, the Enneagram would have remained behind closed doors, stunting both its impact on the world at large and its maturation into a fully holistic tool for transformation.

MORE ABOUT THE SYMBOL

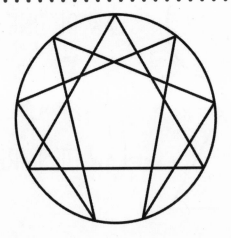

When Gurdjieff brought the symbol of the Enneagram to the Western world, he taught it as sacred geometry. For Gurdjieff, the Enneagram was a map of how energy became manifest in the physical world. It showed how all things came into being and how we are all in a constant state of becoming. While he never specifically spoke of personality typing, the Enneagram was central to the teaching of his particular style of inner personal and spiritual work. Gurdjieff found within the Enneagram what he believed to be the three most important laws of the universe: the law of one, the law of three, and the law of seven, symbolized by the circle, the triangle, and the hexad, respectively. Gurdjieff went as far as to say, "A man may be quite alone in the desert and he can trace the Enneagram in the sand and in it read the eternal laws of the universe. And every time he can learn something new, something he did not know before."*

---

* P. D. Ouspensky, *In Search of the Miraculous: The Teachings of G. I. Gurdjieff* (Boston: Mariner Books, 2001), 301.

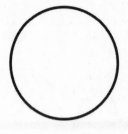

LAW OF ONE

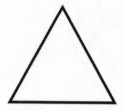

LAW OF THREE

LAW OF SEVEN

The Circle: The outer circle of the Enneagram represents the law of one, which can be understood as the law of oneness. This circle shows our interconnectedness and our inherent underlying unity. It is common to misconstrue this unity for uniformity or use our inherent oneness to downplay or all-out erase our very real differences. Unity in this sense, though, is a oneness and connectedness that welcomes and celebrates our differences.

The Triangle: The inner triangle that connects points 3, 6, and 9 is symbolic of the law of three. This law in the Gurdjieff tradition illustrates the threefoldness of reality and how three distinct yet interconnected forces must be present to create anything new (this is different from the law of three in the pagan traditions). A first force, or holy affirming force, symbolized by the 3 point on the Enneagram, is the start of any new idea. It is the "yes" energy that generates all things. In response to any first force, there is a second force, or holy denying force, symbolized by the 6 point on the Enneagram, that stands in opposition to the "yes" energy. It is the "no" energy that creates all polarity. This polarity creates an impasse if a third force, or holy reconciling force, doesn't enter the equation. This third force isn't simply a compromise between the first and second forces; it creates something wholly new that transcends and includes all of both the "yes" and the "no."

The Hexad: The remainder of the connected lines within the Enneagram make a shape called a hexad. This, despite having only six points, is symbolic of the law of seven. This refers not to the number of points but rather to specific points this shape connects and in which order. The hexad connects points 1, 4, 2, 8, 5, and 7, and this sequence of numbers is significant because dividing any number (except for seven) by seven gives you this repeating sequence of six numbers. For example, one divided by seven equals 0.142857, two divided by seven equals 0.285714, three divided by seven equals 0.428571, and so on. (To be honest, my mind was *blown* when I first learned this.) Gurdjieff taught the law of seven as the predictable patterns everything from people to plants to the movement of the planets goes through in its development. He aligned the seven steps with the seven notes of the Western major scale and would often refer to different phases of life as octaves. *Ouspensky Today* says,

"Understanding the law of seven is the key to learning how to finish what we start and what to expect along the way."*

THE THREE CENTERS

The Enneagram of personality as well as the school of inner work it stems from both see the human system as being divided into three distinct, yet interconnected, ways of taking in, processing, and acting on information and experiences. These are called the Centers of Intelligence, and we base much of what we learn about ourselves in the Enneagram on these three ways of experiencing the world. Understanding what each center does for us will help us see ourselves more clearly and make it easier to bring ourselves and our centers back into balance.

The Body Center is concerned with our autonomy, our own personal rhythms, our Instinctual Drives, and our intuition. Our will and ability to take action are housed in the Body Center, and we use it to manage the outside world—making it "the way it should be"—as well as to manage our own discomfort. The Body Center is where we experience and manage our anger when we perceive threats to our physical safety, position in the world, self-worth, or getting what we want. Dr. David Daniels describes the skill sets of the Body Center as our kinesthetic abilities, physical sensations, and gut instincts or intuitive knowing. All of these directly relate to how we move in the world. When

---

* "The Law of Seven," accessed April 14, 2020, https://www.ouspensky today.org/wp/about-teaching-today/the-law-of-seven/.

functioning at its best, the Body Center expresses a zest for being alive; a feeling of being grounded, solid, and embodied fully in the world; knowing the right amount of energy or power to accomplish tasks; and an understanding of what is ours to do or how to take right action.

The Heart Center is concerned with our emotional experiences, our sense of connection, and our relationships. The Heart Center is where we experience our feelings and is responsible for our emotional expression. It's focused on managing our sadness and grief when we perceive or experience threats to our connection to important others in our lives. We use our Heart Centers to navigate the relational landscape and gain recognition, appreciation, love, and respect to satisfy our need for connection, contact, and approval. Dr. David Daniels describes the skill sets of the Heart Center as the ability to observe moods / feeling states in self and others, adjust internal perspectives to match audience, and adapt to multiple agendas. All of these directly affect how we experience our feelings and emotions and how we relate to others. When the Heart Center is fully functional, it expresses the higher qualities of emotional maturity, empathy, understanding, compassion, and loving-kindness.

The Head Center is concerned with making sense of data and information and securing our own safety and security. It's focused on gaining information to manage the fear and anxiety we feel when we perceive threats to that security. We use our Head Centers to gain a sense of certainty and to help ourselves feel secure in moving forward in our lives. This is where we learn to make decisions and plan for our future. Dr. David Daniels describes the skill sets of the Head Center as the ability to analyze situations and information, figure things out, envision, imagine, and plan. As the Head Center becomes fully developed, it expresses the higher qualities of wisdom, insight, thoughtfulness, and greater knowing.

WHAT IS TYPE? AND WHAT ELSE IS THERE?

As we dive into the Enneagram of personality, it is especially helpful to understand what we're talking about when we talk about "type," as there are many different approaches to this. My definition of type, and the definition that guides all of the information in this book, draws on the Gurdjieffian understanding of personality as well as my own understanding of both Western and Eastern schools of thought in the world of both philosophy and psychology and my own lived experience. Type is simply a set of patterned ways of thinking, feeling, and taking action in the world that have developed over time to meet a person's needs. There is a nearly endless argument about whether type is acquired or inborn (nature vs. nurture), and from what I can tell, it's most likely some cosmic combination of the two. Many teachers believe that babies are born with a "temperament" or what could be seen as the foundation of a person's type, and then a combination of environmental factors such as family of origin, culture, and personal experiences will shape and solidify the personality over the first five to seven years of a child's life.

In many personal and spiritual growth circles, personality is seen as something negative—something to be overcome, transcended, or even destroyed. But Gurdjieff saw personality as something absolutely essential. Without a strong and fully developed personality, Gurdjieff believed there was nothing for our "essence" to feed off. Having a strong personality, while also learning how to move outside of it, was key in his work, and I've found it to be equally valuable in my own personal experience. Personality or type is not merely something that obscures our essential nature (although that can happen); it is also a vehicle for us to bring our essential nature out into the world and express our particular and specific gifts. For this reason, I often find the "type/essence" dichotomy extremely unhelpful. Instead, I think of our journey not from type or personality to some egoless existence but from unconscious thinking, feeling, and moving in the world to conscious thinking, feeling, and moving in the world. When we are acting unconsciously, we are slaves to our patterns and our type. When we are acting consciously, we find the peace, serenity, humility, honesty, equanimity, nonattachment, courage, freedom, and innocence that we've been craving.

The Narrative Enneagram has a similar and very helpful way of describing type with the ideas of expansion and contraction. When the life force or energy in a person is contracted, they are acting from their type, and when the life force or energy of a person is expansive and flowing, they have access to other ways of thinking, feeling, and moving in the world. This contraction and expansion of the life force takes on different characteristics in each center, which creates our Habit of Attention and higher idea in the Head Center, our Habit of Emotion and higher emotional state in the Heart Center, and distorted or life-giving instincts and movement in the Body Center. With this, it's important to note the difference between behaviors and energy. Behaviors have no intrinsic value in this system. It's not about what you do; it's about *how* you do it. Like I mentioned at the beginning of this book, growth isn't about not looking like your type but about becoming more conscious or using a different energy for the things you do.

CONTRACTED

EXPANSIVE

HABIT OF
ATTENTION

HIGHER
(OR HOLY)
IDEA

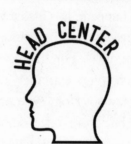

HABIT OF
EMOTION

HIGHER
EMOTIONAL
STATE

DISTORTED
INSTINCTS

LIFE-GIVING
INSTINCTS

CONTRACTED/
UNCONSCIOUS
MOVEMENT

CONSCIOUS
MOVEMENT/
FREEDOM OF
MOVEMENT

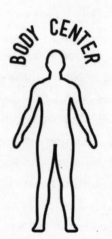

THE NINE TYPES

• •

Type 1

Nicknames: The Reformer / The Perfectionist / The Improver

Base Triad: Body/Instinctual Triad

Stance: Compliant

Harmony Group: Idealist

Dominant Center: Body/Instinctual

Repressed Center: Head/Thinking

Habit of Attention: Being good, doing the right thing, critical thinking, creating order, correcting errors

Higher Idea: Holy Perfection, the realization that all things are unfolding exactly as they should and that there is no need to "correct" them, only the need to show up as yourself and let that be enough

Habit of Emotion: Anger—it shows up as resentment, irritation, and a need to control their emotions

Higher Emotional State: Serenity, the emotional state 1s experience when letting go of their need to control and overmanage situations

Instinctual Habits: Rhythmicity, seeking creating order; strong but highly controlled bodily energy; tension held in the jaw, neck, shoulders, and belly

Defense System:

Idealization: Being good or right

Avoidance: Being wrong, bad, or inappropriate

Defense Mechanism: Reaction Formation

Type 1s are driven by the need to be right or good. Their attention is focused on correcting errors and improving themselves, others, or situations. They deal mostly with anger that shows up in their lives as irritation and resentment. Type 1s are idealists at heart and are willing to put in the work to make things exactly right. They can sometimes come off as harsh or critical to other people, but that is often only because they are dealing with their own overbearing inner critic.

What They See

Type 1s are always striving to be the best. They not only want to do the right thing; they want to be a good person. They seek to correct errors and put things in their proper place. They seek to align themselves with some sort of higher order or ideal and won't rest until they've achieved perfection. Type 1s' critical mind and attention to detail mean they don't settle for less than 100 percent, and that means these are the people we need building our bridges and doing the calculations to send astronauts into space (really, any time things need to be *perfect*).

What They Miss

Because 1s are always comparing things to an ideal they hold within themselves, they often miss the ways in which things are working out *more perfectly* than they anticipated. They have also blinded themselves to their own anger because, let's face it, anger isn't good, and 1s have to be good. Leaving their anger under wraps means that it can seep out as irritation and resentment, which promise to be far more damaging to relationships than anger expressed honestly. The real catch for 1s is that their desire to help others be better often comes off as harsh and critical, making the relationships they're trying to improve more strained.

Their Work

The work for 1s starts on the inside. Self-acceptance and mindful self-compassion are earth-shattering practices for the 1. Being in the Body Triad, finding enough space to practice these things will be hard without some physical practice first. Yoga and meditation are great tools for 1s to relax into the serenity that's waiting for them past their judging mind.

Type 2

Nicknames: The Helper / The Giver

Base Triad: Heart/Emotional Triad

Stance: Compliant

Harmony Group: Relationist

Dominant Center: Heart/Emotional

Repressed Center: Head/Thinking

Habit of Attention: The needs and feelings of others, earning recognition and approval, making relationships "work"

Higher Idea: Holy Will, the understanding that the universe, divine, spirit, source, and so on will meet the needs of all people in the right measure and time, and it's not the job of the 2 to meet them

Habit of Emotion: Pride—it shows up as an inflated or deflated self-worth depending on the approval of others and in the belief that they don't have needs

Higher Emotional State: Humility, the emotional state experienced when 2s admit their needs and allow themselves to be seen in their neediness

Instinctual Habits: High in empathy, responsive, moves out toward others, breath is habitually pushed into chest, tends toward breathlessness

Defense System:

    Idealization: Being helpful/needed

    Avoidance: Feeling needy or helpless

    Defense Mechanism: Repression

Type 2s are driven by the need to be helpful or even indispensable. They are warm and affectionate and are keenly aware of the needs of others. They deal mostly with shame and work to overcome it by becoming helpful and endearing themselves to others. Their attention is habitually focused on other people, and often this causes them to lose sight of themselves and their own needs.

What They See
Type 2s are deeply relational, and their attention is always focused on how to make their relationships work and work better. They have an ability to sense the needs and feelings of others and work to meet those needs and tend to those feelings. Type 2s work tirelessly to support those they love and often know what others need before they do. They use this skill to try to earn the love and acceptance they crave. Naturally caring and empathetic, 2s' energy is warm and inviting, and they bring a positive feeling wherever they go.

What They Miss
With their focus firmly on other people, 2s often miss out on what they feel/need/want themselves. This leads to an experience of pride, assuming that because they don't see any of their needs, they must not have them. They can also experience an inflated or deflated sense of self-worth depending on their external approval rating. Type 2s can lose themselves reaching toward others and even "help themselves to death." In average or unhealthy ranges, they engage in "give-to-get" kinds of helping and end up frustrated that others aren't holding up their end of the deal, causing rifts in the relationships 2s value most.

Their Work

Type 2s work lies in self-inquiry and self-examination. They need to get in touch with their own needs and turn that amazing nurturing energy on themselves for a little while or, better yet, allow someone else to help them and meet their needs for a change (*gasp!*). This practice of humility brings a healing balance to the important relationships in the 2's life.

Type 3

Nicknames: The Achiever / The Performer / The Chameleon

Base Triad: Heart/Emotional Triad

Stance: Assertive

Harmony Group: Pragmatist

Dominant Center: Heart/Emotional

Repressed Center: Heart/Emotional

Habit of Attention: Goals, tasks, getting things done, achievements, maintaining positive image, potential, and value

Higher Idea: Holy Hope, the understanding that one does not need to strive or achieve in order to be worthy of love and belonging

Habit of Emotion: Deceit—it shows up as the belief that they are the persona they project into the world

Higher Emotional State: Truthfulness or honesty, being true to who they are and nonidentifying with their persona

Instinctual Habits: High activity levels, has "go-forward" energy, breathes more into the chest, has a tendency to overwork and overexert, highly adaptable

Defense System:

Idealization: Being successful

Avoidance: Failing

Defense Mechanism: Identification

Type 3s are driven by a need to be successful and achieve the goals they've set for themselves. Their attention is focused on tasks and their own accomplishments. They most often deal with shame, although they have repressed this feeling in favor of earning their worth through success and achievement. Type 3s know how to get the job done in the most efficient way possible and take little time to celebrate their own success. They are prone to burnout, and if they aren't careful, they may cut corners to be the first to cross the finish line. While their focus is on "success," success looks different for every 3. Type 3s often mistype as the type they deem the most appropriate for their environment or personal goals.

What They See
Type 3s have an ability to get things done as efficiently as possible. They have a deep desire to be seen as successful. They are image-focused, meaning they are tuned in to how they are coming across to others, and they want to meet and exceed the expectations of others. Type 3s are extremely hard workers and know how to read a room and shift themselves accordingly to maximize success. Type 3s have an inherent ability to see the true potential and value of everything they come into contact with. Their drive and ambition show us the quickest way forward to a new and beautiful future.

What They Miss
Type 3s have lost the message that love is not something that is earned through what you do but is freely given to you because of who you are. They often miss out on their own personal experiences and inner world because of their laser

focus on the outer world and trying to be successful. Type 3s are usually not available for the depth of intimate connection available to them because of their constant drive to move forward. Without these deep, intimate connections, the success that they believe will win them love and affection leaves them feeling empty.

Their Work

The 3s' work is to slow down and find the connection, validation, and meaning they're looking for in the world around them inside themselves. Type 3s may never rid themselves of their goal orientation (and they certainly don't need to), but it can be helpful to focus on setting goals that have a benefit for more than just themselves and bring more meaning and value into their lives.

Type 4

Nicknames: The Romantic / The Individualist / The Artist

Base Triad: Heart/Emotional Triad

Stance: Withdrawn

Harmony Group: Idealist

Dominant Center: Heart/Emotional

Repressed Center: Body/Instinctual

Habit of Attention: What's missing; personal authenticity; the "reality" underneath the surface of things; what is unique, novel, or creative

Higher Idea: Holy Origin, the understanding that we are all inextricably linked to one another from our common origin from source, spirit, God, and so on

Habit of Emotion: Envy—it most often shows up as a desire for the ease and comfort that others seem to have in moving through the world as well as a general sense of longing

Higher Emotional State: Equanimity, the emotional state of being deeply grounded and settled despite what emotional content may be playing out on the surface

Instinctual Habits: High emotional sensitivity, intense feelings that shift frequently, seeks both contact and privacy, often breathes more into the belly

Defense System:

    Idealization: Being unique, authentic, special

    Avoidance: Being ordinary or inauthentic

    Defense Mechanism: Introjection

Type 4s are driven by the need to be special or unique. Their attention is habitually drawn to what is missing in any given situation. They are deep and often moody, keenly aware of their own emotional state. They deal mostly with sadness and shame and are comfortable sitting with their own melancholy. Type 4s are creative and expressive, and while not all 4s are artists in the traditional sense, they bring their own aesthetic into everything they do. They have trouble being present to what good things they have in the moment, as they often lose themselves in nostalgia.

What They See

Type 4s are driven to be authentic. They have a flair for the dramatic that brings an energy and intensity to every-thing they do. Because of their focus on what is not there, 4s experience a deep and almost constant state of longing. Often 4s are creative and stylish and like to be seen as such but aren't overly concerned with being "liked" by others. They are searching for depth and meaning in their work and relationships and can't stand to be stuck on the surface of things. Type 4s have no trouble plumbing the depths of their darker emotions and have an innate ability to help others do the same.

What They Miss

In always seeing what's missing in any given situation, 4s can often miss what's actually there. Like their 1 counterparts, they have set an internalized ideal as something to be achieved and experience extreme disappointment when life doesn't measure up. Type 4s experience their emotions as the core of who they are and can easily be swept away by the mood of the moment. Often 4s will shy away from the happier and lighter side of the emotional spectrum because it doesn't feel real enough, which leads them to wallow in their melancholy.

Their Work

Type 4s' work is to develop a more grounded presence. This is often achieved through getting more in touch with their bodies. As 4s learn to identify less with their emotions and more as a holistic being, they experience a sense of equanimity. Their emotions may still be moving and shaking on the inside, but 4s won't be taken for a ride.

Type 5

Nicknames: The Investigator / The Observer

Base Triad: Head/Intellectual Triad

Stance: Withdrawn

Harmony Group: Relationist

Dominant Center: Head/Thinking

Repressed Center: Body/Instinctual

Habit of Attention: Gaining knowledge, developing expertise, understanding systems and phenomena, protecting privacy and autonomy

Higher Idea: Holy Omniscience, knowing that true understanding doesn't come from hoarding knowledge but rather comes from aligning oneself with the flow of all knowledge and wisdom

Habit of Emotion: Avarice—it shows up as a holding back and holding on to resources, information, and especially their personal experience

Higher Emotional State: Nonattachment, the willingness to let all things come and go as they will without attaching to them or avoiding them

Instinctual Habits: Highly sensitive nervous system, easily overwhelmed by stimuli or interpersonal contact, breath is often in the belly, and there is a pattern of underbreathing

Defense System:

Idealization: Understanding, being knowledgeable

Avoidance: Being incompetent, emptiness

Defense Mechanism: Isolation

Type 5s are driven by a need to know or understand. They are focused on gaining knowledge and information. Type 5s prefer to sit on the sidelines and observe from a distance before engaging in new activities or situations. They deal mostly with fear and anxiety, generally relating to feeling incompetent, unprepared, or depleted. Type 5s have strong boundaries and are particularly averse to emotional intrusion. They are often extremely knowledgeable and come into relationships without an agenda. Type 5s have trouble taking the information they've gathered and taking necessary action around it.

What They See

Well, what don't they see? Type 5s tend to stand on the outskirts of things and observe from a distance, and they are *very* observant. They have a strong desire to gain knowledge and expertise and seek to "corner the market" on information about the topics they love. Type 5s love systems and organizing information, so they are always prepared for any intellectual gunfight that might ensue. They are deeply concerned with their own personal autonomy and seek to be as self-sufficient as possible. Type 5s embody the hermit archetype, storing up wisdom and knowledge, and at their best they are generous with what they know and what they have and can put their great ideas into action.

What They Miss

Type 5s focus all of their attention and energy into their heads, often leaving their hearts and bodies sorely neglected. In their quest for deep understanding, they can become emotionally detached and lose connection with the world around them. While their need for autonomy keeps them individuated, it also isolates them. Their continued focus on gaining more and better information runs on a loop and prevents them from taking effective action with the knowledge they have. It's been said that knowledge applied is wisdom, and 5s thirst for wisdom, but they miss out by not applying the knowledge they already have and continually searching for more.

Their Work

Type 5s spend their time in their heads, but they need to journey down into their hearts if they want to have the meaningful emotional experiences that make life worth living. That's not an easy task for a 5, though. Instead of going headfirst (Ha! See what I did there?) into the heart, body work is an amazing way for 5s to become more comfortable in their own skin and therefore more comfortable with their emotions. Yoga is very popular among 5s because of its philosophical connections. They just need to make sure they take their practice into community so as not to let it increase their isolation.

Type 6

Nicknames: The Loyal Skeptic / Devil's Advocate / The Buddy

Base Triad: Head/Intellectual Triad

Stance: Compliant

Harmony Group: Pragmatist

Dominant Center: Head/Thinking

Repressed Center: Head/Thinking

Habit of Attention: Anticipating problems and finding solutions; worst-case-scenario planning; figuring things out; rebelling against or challenging structures, systems, or ideas; developing new structures, systems, or ideas

Higher Idea: Holy Faith, the belief that everything will work out for the best, even without constant planning and strife

Habit of Emotion: Fear—it shows up as anxiety and a search for security or certainty, can also manifest as aggression and pushback as a counterphobic movement

Higher Emotional State: Courage, the heart's capacity to experience and hold fear without allowing it to disrupt the balanced functioning of the Head, Heart, and Body Centers

Instinctual Habits: Highly sensitive nervous system, acts as a security system ready to sound the alarm, easily agitated, overactive fight/flight/

freeze response, tends toward breathlessness and unconsciously holds
the breath

Defense System:
Idealization: Feeling certain, secure; being loyal
Avoidance: Being unsafe, insecure, or disloyal
Defense Mechanism: Projection

Type 6s are driven by a need to be secure. Their focus is
on outer authority, and they can either submit themselves to
it wholeheartedly or push against it in rebellion. They have
questioning minds and often seek out second, third, and
fourth opinions. They deal mostly with fear and anxiety,
having lost touch with their own inner guidance. Type 6s are
loyal and devoted friends who are always prepared in a crisis. They have trouble with overthinking and can get caught
up in worst-case-scenario planning.

What They See

Type 6s have a finely tuned eye for seeing what could go
wrong in situations. They can anticipate problems and find
solutions. Type 6s are driven to always be prepared for any
contingency. They are well equipped to both develop and
challenge ideas, structures, and systems. They desire to be
deeply loyal to worthy people and groups. Type 6s at their best
are the glue that holds organizations together and can also
be effective leaders.

What They Miss

Type 6s have lost touch with their own inner guidance and
authority, and because of this, they seek out guidance
and authority from others. This creates a lack of faith or

trust in themselves that they project onto other people. This leads to the 6s pushing and testing their relationships—be it at home, at work, or with friends—and can often create a self-fulfilling prophesy. The 6s' questioning mind is a wonderful asset when used appropriately, but when it's running the show, it can undermine the relationships that 6s hold dear.

Their Work

Type 6s have to tap into their own inner knowing and guidance. While this proves to be their greatest struggle, once they learn to tune in, listen, and follow their inner voice, everything about their life changes for the better. Before that giant goal is achieved, though, it can be helpful for the 6 to practice making a decision (even if they don't have all the answers) and moving forward without the self-doubt and second-guessing.

Type 7

Nicknames: The Enthusiast / The Epicure / The Adventurer

Base Triad: Head/Intellectual Triad

Stance: Assertive

Harmony Group: Idealist

Dominant Center: Head/Thinking

Repressed Center: Heart/Feeling

Habit of Attention: Future planning, multiple options and possibilities, positivity, what is enjoyable in life

Higher Idea: Holy Work, the ability to keep the mind focused even when things become difficult, uncomfortable, or painful

Habit of Emotion: Gluttony—it shows up as fear of limitation, craving more (of life, experience, etc.), fear of missing out

Higher Emotional State: Constancy, the heart's capacity to stay with and experience all emotions, even those that may be uncomfortable or painful

Instinctual Habits: High energy, in need of constant stimulation, bodily energy moves up toward the head and forward, high capacity for stimulation and personal contact

Defense System:

Idealization: Being free

Avoidance: Being limited, being trapped in pain

Defense Mechanism: Rationalization

Type 7s are driven by a need to avoid pain or discomfort. Their attention is focused on possibilities and positive future planning. They deal mostly with fear and anxiety, but they distract themselves from it through their many fun and enjoyable experiences. Type 7s strongly dislike feeling trapped or limited in any way. They are fun and energetic and are masters of finding silver linings. They can miss out on meaningful experiences in life because of their drive to not feel pain either physically or emotionally.

What They See

Type 7s are all about living an enjoyable life. They keep their eyes on the future and like to keep their options open. They have an uncanny ability to see the possibilities and excellent potential in all things. They are fantastic planners and want to always stay ahead of the game. Type 7s are incredibly high energy and are always on the lookout for the next big adventure, sometimes even before the adventure they're on is over. Type 7s have an almost magical ability to see the positive in even the darkest of situations, and their energy and excitement for life bring joy wherever they go.

What They Miss

With their energy always moving forward, 7s may have the hardest time being present of any of the types. If they overuse their gift of finding silver linings, they can come off as shallow, aloof, and emotionally distant, making it hard to sustain the more meaningful intimate relationships that emotional presence facilitates. In their search for more (of basically everything), they can miss out on the beauty and value of what's in front of them, ensuring that they always feel that looming sense of lack and limitation. Their ever-positive outlook leaves little room for the darker or heavier side of the emotional spectrum, which can keep them from developing into emotional maturity.

Their Work

Type 7s have to learn and experience that sadness won't kill them. Neither will pain, discomfort, or any of a long list of less-than-happy emotions. To do this, though, they need to slow down and funnel some of their energy into their heart space. This is difficult without consistent, disciplined practice, and since that isn't the 7s' strong suit, finding a way to make their practices like yoga and meditation fun and enjoyable will be important. Often having someone to keep them accountable makes the largest impact.

Type 8

Nicknames: The Challenger / The Protector / The Boss
Base Triad: Body/Instinctual Triad
Stance: Assertive
Harmony Group: Relationist
Dominant Center: Body/Instinctual

Repressed Center: Heart/Feeling

Habit of Attention: Fairness, justice, vengeance, personal empowerment, taking action, meeting and creating conflict as necessary

Higher Idea: Holy Truth, experiencing the deeper truth in a situation often aligned with seeing the humanity in others

Habit of Emotion: Lust—it shows up as intensity, immediacy, urgency, anger, and avoiding vulnerability

Higher Emotional State: Innocence, the heart's ability to welcome circumstances and emotions as they are without needing to intensify or control them

Instinctual Habits: Strong, go-forward energy; intensity in response to most if not all things; enjoys pushing against obstacles; excess is work, play, and consumption

Defense System:

    Idealization: Being strong, being unaffected

    Avoidance: Being weak, being vulnerable

    Defense Mechanism: Denial

Type 8s are driven by a need to be strong. Their attention is habitually turned to their own personal empowerment and expressing their power in the world. They deal most with anger and are often seen as aggressive or overbearing. They are deeply intolerant of injustice and are defenders of the underdogs. Type 8s are powerful, charismatic, and natural leaders. They can be emotionally insensitive to others and are often out of touch with their own softer emotions.

What They See

Type 8s are tuned into power: who has it, who doesn't, and how it's being used. They keep an eye out for the underdogs and have no tolerance for injustice. Type 8s are preoccupied by their own personal empowerment and then seek to empower others. They are deeply motivated to have an impact on their surroundings and are always ready to take action, even if it means engaging in conflict. Type 8s are always ready for a battle, but they're going to make damn sure it's a level playing field for everyone involved. At their best, 8s are magnanimous and heroic leaders who are willing to sacrifice themselves for those they love.

What They Miss

With their focus so keyed into their own personal power, 8s tend to shy away from acknowledging any of their softer, more vulnerable parts. This often means that 8s are out of tune with their own emotional landscapes and therefore have difficulty dealing with others' emotions as well. This lack of emotional connection is the 8s' biggest challenge. If 8s aren't careful, they end up leading groups to suppress the feeling that they can't *truly* be a part of them. This creates the potential for miscommunication: 8s see themselves as loving and dutiful, while the ones they love can see them as demanding, controlling, or bullying.

Their Work

Type 8s need to slow down enough to get in touch with their own emotions and make the time and space to be present for others' emotions as well. Rigorous but mindful exercise is often necessary to burn off excess bodily energy before they can move into the stillness and softening they desperately need.

Type 9

Nicknames: The Peacemakers / The Mediators

Base Triad: Body/Instinctual Triad

Stance: Withdrawn

Harmony Group: Pragmatist

Dominant Center: Body/Instinctual

Repressed Center: Body/Instinctual

Habit of Attention: Avoiding or mediating conflict, peace, harmony, personal comfort, dispersed or diffused attention, difficulty focusing and prioritizing

Higher Idea: Holy Love, the reciprocal care and concern that flows between all beings and the earth itself

Habit of Emotion: Sloth—it shows up as self-forgetting, personal and spiritual listlessness, surrender to inertia, and being unwilling and stubborn

Higher Emotional State: Right Action, the ability to do what is rightfully yours to do while being unattached to the outcome

Instinctual Habits: Adaptability, self-soothing and self-calming, breath is focused in the belly, has low tolerance and capacity for personal needs, desires, and priorities

Defense System:

Idealization: Being peaceful, harmonious

Avoidance: Being in conflict

Defense Mechanism: Narcotization

Type 9s are driven by a need to be peaceful and harmonious. Their attention is often diffused, and they can have trouble focusing on any one particular thing. They are brilliant mediators and have a gift for seeing and understanding both sides to any argument. They struggle most with anger, forgetting it for months or even years at a time only to have it resurface in an explosive way later. Type 9s are kind, gentle, and easygoing. They often have trouble speaking up for their own needs and desires, keeping quiet in favor of "keeping the peace."

What They See

Type 9s, having their place at the tip-top of the Enneagram, have a knack for seeing all sides of an issue. They are driven to create and experience peace and harmony in their lives and in the world around them. Type 9s are gifted therapists and mediators because of their ability to create space for other people and make them feel seen, heard, and validated. They believe that all conflict can be resolved. Honestly, if it weren't for the 9s in the world right now, we probably would have all died in a nuclear holocaust already.

What They Miss

With their keen focus on keeping the peace, 9s often miss out on their own thoughts, feelings, and desires for fear of creating or experiencing conflict. Type 9s avoid conflict like the plague, and since conflict is an inevitable part of life on this planet, they will often remove themselves, either emotionally or physically, from their own life. In their haste to smooth over the conflict they do experience, they can short-change themselves and those they love by not letting the real desires and emotions of the situation surface.

Their Work

The real work for 9s is first getting in touch with what they truly want and need. This often looks like getting in touch with their long-dormant anger. Getting comfortable with anger is a slow and scary process for 9s, but once they make friends with their anger, they can channel it to fuel real and meaningful engagement in their own lives. Type 9s need to know what they want and stand up for it in order to know the true meaning of harmony.

TRIAD BREAKDOWNS

The Enneagram, being a system of nine types, is triadic in nature, meaning that things are continually broken down into three groups of three—it's really quite handy. These triads are organized by how each type sees or works with certain issues or Centers of Intelligence. Each type shares at least one triad with every other type, which reinforces our connectedness and shared humanity.

Dominant Center or Base Triads (8, 9, 1; 2, 3, 4; 5, 6, 7)

Each of us has three Centers of Intelligence that we use to process information and experiences: head, heart, and body. As we develop, we begin to spend more of our time and energy with one specific center and leave the others behind. Which center we lead with, or which center we use first and use most often, will determine certain aspects of our type structure that our type will share with two other types. These groupings are most often referred to as the triads, but because we'll be discussing a few different types of triads, we'll refer to these as the Base Triads.

People in the Body Base Triad (8, 9, 1) are what traditional Enneagram wisdom calls the self-forgetting types. Each of these three types forget some crucial aspect of their

BASE TRIADS

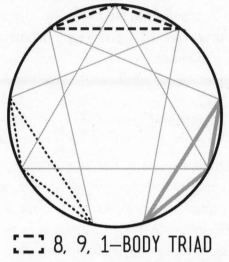

⎡_⎤ 8, 9, 1—BODY TRIAD
☐ 2, 3, 4—HEART TRIAD
⎡⋯⎤ 5, 6, 7—HEAD TRIAD

own humanity, and because of this, they deal mostly with anger. One type outwardly and easily expresses anger, one internalizes their anger, and the other forgets their anger. Body Base Triad types are concerned with fairness and justice and are action oriented. They take in information and read the world through their gut instincts. They are often stubborn, willful, and concerned with the task at hand, even if it's not the task that is theirs to do. These types, after working through their anger, are shining examples of true compassion.

The Heart Base Triad types (2, 3, 4) are referred to as the feeling or connection types. Each of these types is concerned with the heart-based connection they have with other people, and they deal mostly with the sadness and shame at their perceived disconnection. One type manages shame through making themselves invaluable by helping and doing good deeds; one type manages shame through achievements, accomplishments, and shifting themselves to be seen as valuable by their audience; and the other manages shame through setting themselves apart in uniqueness or specialness. These types can often be seen as moody or over the top and place too much of their personal self-esteem in the approval of others. As these types deal with the shame and sadness they experience, they become the true benchmarks of self-confidence and self-worth.

Types in the Head Base Triad (5, 6, 7) are called the mental or planning types. Each of these types is focusing on planning and preparing to assuage the fear and anxiety they experience because of their perceived lack of security or safety. One type focuses on gaining knowledge and addresses this anxiety through making themselves competent, one type deals with anxiety by imagining worst-case scenarios and developing plans to allow themselves to feel prepared, and one type seemingly forgets their fear and focuses on positive future planning. These types are prone to overthinking and can easily become lost in "analysis paralysis." As these types deal with and work through their fear, they can teach the rest of us what true courage looks like.

Conflict Resolution Styles (1, 3, 5; 2, 7, 9; 4, 6, 8)

Conflict is unavoidable, and each personality style has developed its own way of dealing with this inevitable part of life. While each type deals with conflict in its own way, there are similarities among types that can be mapped and

CONFLICT RESOLUTION STYLES

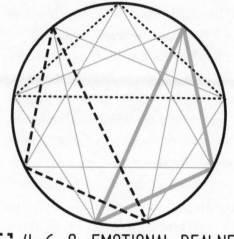

⌐⌐⌐ 4, 6, 8—EMOTIONAL REALNESS
▢ 1, 3, 5—COMPETENCY
⌐...⌐ 2, 7, 9—POSITIVE OUTLOOK

categorized in another three triads. We call these triads the Conflict Resolution Styles. Each style has its strengths and weaknesses in dealing with conflict, and it's important to remember that one style is not better than any of the others. By understanding our personal approach to conflict and learning about the other two, we can be more open to resolving conflicts by using all three styles. The Conflict Resolution Styles are also referred to in some of the Enneagram literature as the Harmonic Groups, but seeing as we'll also be discussing the Harmony Groups in the Enneagram, I find it much easier to stick with Conflict Resolution Styles.

Types 1, 3, and 5 are considered the Competency Types. When faced with a conflict, their approach seems cool, even calculated, as they remove themselves from the emotional material of the conflict and seek to process it in a way that is considered appropriate and rational. These three types are looking for the solution to the problem and want to keep the problem from happening again. This approach to conflict is often considered the more "mature" approach, but without getting to the emotional truth of the conflict or being able to reframe in order to see the positive aspects of what's going on, these types often come off as cold or unfeeling, overly pessimistic, and too concerned with being "right" or winning the argument.

Type 2s, 7s, and 9s are in the Positive Outlook Triad. These types are conditioned to find the silver lining in whatever conflict they find themselves in. Their goal is to smooth things over and make sure everyone is "OK." These types are quick to move through conflict and don't like to dwell in the "negative" energy that conflict creates. Their ability to see the positives and help people move through conflict can be the antidote to those types who see everything as a problem to be fixed or want to keep themselves caught in the emotional turmoil that conflict can bring. Yet without balancing their approach, the Positive Outlook types can be seen as shallow and often develop poor boundaries.

Types 4, 6, and 8 are known as the Emotional Realness Triad or the Emotional Truth Tellers. These types seek to resolve conflict by getting down to the nitty-gritty emotional truth of the situation. They seek to clear the air and get down to brass tacks, believing that if both sides of the conflict are fully heard and seen, resolution will be inevitable. The Emotional Realness group does a great job of cutting through the cultural niceties that can obscure the origin of the conflict and gaining a clear understanding of the humanity of all of the participants. If 8s, 4s, and 6s can't balance their approach with the other two styles, though, they may find themselves dwelling too much in the negative aspects of the situations or unable to see the clear solutions to their problems.

Hornevian Groups (1, 2, 6; 4, 5, 9; 7, 8, 3)

The Hornevian groups are based around the work of developmental psychologist Karen Horney. Horney found that children develop different ways of attaching to or relating to the people around them by moving toward other people, moving away from other people, or moving against other people. While we are all capable of moving in any of these directions, our type will determine which direction we tend to move most often. This is also correlated to which center of intelligence we have the least amount of access to, or which center we use the least.

Compliant Triad (1, 2, 6): The three types who move toward others are in the Compliant Triad. These are people who comply with social standards and norms and are deeply aware of the expectations of others, actively seeking to meet those expectations. These people are deeply loyal and dependable but can often struggle with codependency. They can be overcome by bouts of perfectionism and are particularly susceptible to imposter syndrome. The Compliant Triad is associated with a repressed Head Center. This doesn't mean that people in this triad don't have thoughts or are unintelligent—what it means is that their thought processes are often *unproductive*. One type is habitually caught in self-criticism, one type is habitually looking for what could

HORNEVIAN GROUPS

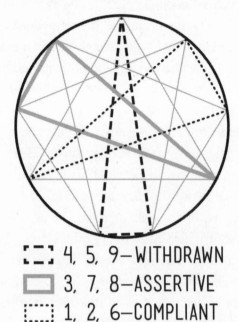

⌐¬ 4, 5, 9—WITHDRAWN

▭ 3, 7, 8—ASSERTIVE

⌐⌐ 1, 2, 6—COMPLIANT

go wrong in situations, and one type is habitually concerned with the feelings and needs of others.

Withdrawn Triad (4, 5, 9): Those who move away from people belong to the Withdrawn Triad. These are people who seek to meet their own needs by retreating inward away from people, situations, and conflict. These people have a rich and interesting inner life and genuinely enjoy their own company. They can be introverted and shy and particularly slow to take action. These types have repressed their Body or Gut Center, which obviously doesn't mean that they don't have a body but rather that they are out of touch with their gut instincts, will, and self-confidence. These types may have a particularly difficult time with executing the projects they've dreamed up in their heads. One type will never feel intellectually prepared enough to start, one type will start with fervor but abandon the project as their emotional experience of it shifts, and the other type struggles to set themselves as a priority in their own life, letting the projects and priorities of others take center stage.

Assertive Triad (3, 7, 8): The three types who move against others are in the Assertive Triad. These people are highly energetic and often very positive. These are high-energy types who are concerned with taking action and moving things forward. They are natural and comfortable leaders, and we often look to them for advice and guidance because of their ability to get things done. These types are often impatient and impulsive and have been described as insensitive. The assertive stance is associated with a repressed Heart Center. Just as in the other two stances, this does not mean these types don't have hearts or feelings, but that they don't give attention to their own feelings and often have trouble relating to the feelings of others. One type denies their feelings and vulnerabilities through being strong, one type keeps themselves always on the move to ward off darker feelings, and one type shifts or performs their emotional experiences to align with those around them.

Harmony Groups (3, 6, 9; 2, 5, 8; 1, 4, 7)

The Harmony Groups are another way of organizing the types by how they view and move through the world. These groups, when outlined on the Enneagram, create three equilateral triangles, and many believe the connections made here help us all find the pieces we've been missing to experience the fullness of our three-centered intelligence. These

HARMONY GROUPS

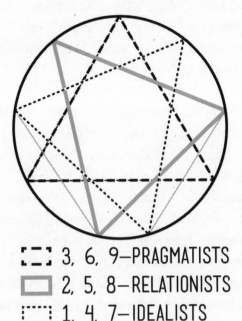

:⁻: 3, 6, 9—PRAGMATISTS
▢ 2, 5, 8—RELATIONISTS
:⁞⁞: 1, 4, 7—IDEALISTS

three triangles show the most natural flow for each type to experience their less developed centers.

Pragmatists (3, 6, 9): Types 3, 6, and 9 create the only equilateral triangle on the Enneagram and not only represent the "core" of each of their respective dominant triads but also represent how we "blend into, align with, and thrive alongside others in the world."* Type 3s represent the ambition that allows humanity to strive for new advancements in all areas of life, 6s represent the caution that is required to fully flesh out and develop new ideas, and 9s represent our

---

* Dr. David Daniels, "Working with the Enneagram Harmony Triads," accessed April 14, 2020, https://drdaviddaniels.com/articles/triads/.

ability to find equilibrium amid change and disruption. Riso and Hudson refer to these types as the attachment types, and Dr. Bill Schafer calls them the "Earth Types" because of how they represent the ways we relate to the world around us in our day-to-day lives.

Relationists (2, 5, 8): These types are called the Relationists because they are the exemplars of the three different ways we can relate to those around us: moving toward, away from, and against. Riso and Hudson refer to these types as the rejection types, as they attempt to stave off rejection through being helpful (type 2), isolating (type 5), or appearing strong or unaffected (type 8). This triangle on the Enneagram is the only place where type 2 is directly connected to any Head Center type. This is where 2s can find a stronger connection to their repressed Head Center in the energy of point 5 on the Enneagram. As 2s learn to step back, gain perspective, and quiet themselves internally, they get in touch with their healthy and balanced intellectual capacity. Dr. Bill Schafer calls these types the "Human Triad" as they are where we develop deep and lasting connections with others.

Idealists (1, 4, 7): These types are called the Idealists because they all look to what "could be" rather than what is. Type 7s see what positive, fun, and enjoyable things lie in the future; 1s are working in the present to manifest a better world; and 4s remain in longing for what's missing, which is often wrapped in nostalgia from the past. Riso and Hudson refer to these types as the frustration types, as all three work to overcome their personal frustration with the way things are. It's in this triangle that 7s find their natural movement into their repressed Heart Center at point 4. As 7s embody more 4 energy by slowing down and staying with difficult, painful, and dark emotions, they find the balance of their emotional center. Dr. Bill Schafer refers to these types as the "Heaven Types," as they are focused on the ultimate possibilities that are beyond the here and now.

The Bermuda Triangle

You may have noticed in the description of the nine types that there are three types whose dominant and repressed center are the same. These are the types that are lovingly referred to as the Bermuda Triangle because they all sit on the inner triangle of the Enneagram. Clearly something strange is going on here! Types 3, 6, and 9 are representative as the "core" type for their dominant triad (3s are the core of the heart types, 6s are the core of the head types, and 9s are the core of the body types), and because of this they have a particular difficulty with their dominant center of intelligence: their dominant center is also their repressed center. What this means for these types out in the world is that, as Peter O'Hanrahan would often say during trainings, "their dominant center is not available for personal use." Or in other words, they are bringing in information and reading the world from their dominant center, but they are habitually and unconsciously responding to this information from their other two Centers of Intelligence.

An 8, for example, reads the world from their gut or Body Center and then responds by taking action (from their Body Center). Their 9 neighbors read the world through their gut in a very similar way, but they don't have the same access to the Body Center to respond from that place, so instead they spend their time thinking or feeling in response to what they read from their gut. Many 9s I've spoken to have shared that if they've thought about something enough, they feel like they've actually done it. While 5s read the world from their Head Center, and then use their intellect to organize the information and make sense of things, 6s read the same information through their Head Center, but then use their bodies and hearts to respond. This causes 6s to respond to new information with an immense amount of anxiety (Heart Center) or to jump into action without thinking things through (Body Center) or some combination of both. Type 2s read the world from their Heart Center, feeling the feelings and emotions of others in a way that touches their own, resulting in a deep empathic resonance with others (note: this isn't always a good thing!). Move clockwise one space to type 3 and you see people who read the world through their hearts in a similar way to 2s but respond much differently. They don't have the same access to their own feelings as 2s do, so they respond to the feelings of others by thinking and doing, using the information they've read from their Heart Center to their advantage.

TYPING: HOW TO *REALLY* FIND YOUR TYPE
. . . .

Most people assume that the first step on an Enneagram journey is to discover our type. But, because the point of this work is to develop and awaken all three of our centers in order to meet life as it comes, it's helpful to start first with our centers and then move on to type. Our type is determined by our core motivations, and these motivations cause certain distortions of our centers. One center will be overused or "dominant," even enlisting the help of our "support" center, while the third center is often ignored or "repressed." If we can gain an understanding of which center we lead with and which one we tend to leave behind, we'll be on a solid path to understanding our type.

To understand your dominant center, we look at the characteristics of the triads. The Enneagram being a system of nine is triadic in nature, and the types relate to each other through different sets of three based on different characteristics. These triads have different names, but the triads based on lead center are often just referred to as the triads. To avoid confusion, I refer to them as the Base Triads, as the center you lead with constitutes the base of your Enneagram type.

Most people can easily see themselves in one of the three Base Triads or at the very least have a strong sense of which one they *aren't*. Take a moment to reflect on your life and notice which of the paragraphs in the triad section above feels the most resonant. Once you can see which center you lead with, it will be time to turn your attention to which center you leave behind—a very tricky task! If we could see what our blind spots are, they wouldn't be our blind spots. Simply looking at the centers and deciding which one you use least is not the most effective strategy.

When I first started in my self-observation and self-awareness work, I could have sworn to you up and down that I was a feeling type. I mean, I cry at commercials if the dog is cute enough. I was certain that I lead with feeling and that doing would have been my least active center, but once I was able to see how the centers really operated, it was clear that my Heart Center was the most removed from my experience. What helped me the most was looking at the triads associated with our repressed centers. Looking at how our repressed centers affect how we show up in the world is something like a side-view mirror. It's something in our eyesight that allows us a little more insight into what's been lurking in our blind spots.

The triads associated with our repressed centers are called the Hornevian Triads or the Stances, depending on which school of Enneagram knowledge you follow. These three triads are related to the three attachment styles developed by Karen Horney, a German-born psychoanalyst who worked in the early and mid-1900s. Horney stated that there were three distinct styles of relating to others that all children try on in order to get their needs met—they either move toward, move away from, or move against. The tendency to habitually move in one of these directions is clearly mapped in the Enneagram.

Just like with the Base Triads, taking some time to reflect on which one of those paragraphs is more resonant will get you another step closer to understanding your type. Use what you've learned about your Base Triad and your Stance to fill in the chart below to see what type you may be. In both my private practice and my teaching, I have found this to be the most reliable way of guiding groups of people into an understanding of their individual types. It is in no way foolproof, but I've found that it tends to bypass a lot of the issues of wishful mistyping and misunderstanding. Once you have an idea of one or two possible types, review the type descriptions and see which resonate the most.

If you're still unsure of which type you lead with, I recommend reaching out to a trained professional to do a typing interview. These interviews are a time for you to explore *you* and have someone come along for the ride who can help make sense of it in terms of the Enneagram. People trained to give typing interviews are not there to diagnose you with a type but rather to help make some things clearer for you by reflecting back things about yourself you may not have been able to see. There is a list of qualified professionals at the back of this book.

FINDING YOUR TYPE

	HEAD	HEART	BODY
COMPLIANT	6	2	1
WITHDRAWN	5	4	9
ASSERTIVE	7	3	8

INSTINCTS AND SUBTYPES

A variety of theories and applications beyond the basics of core type have been born out of the Enneagram. Some I find fascinating, while others seem contrived and offer little in terms of personal and spiritual growth. For the most part, I steer away from them in favor of focusing on more practical and helpful ideas. One of the most important pieces of Enneagram wisdom that goes beyond the types is the work done around the instincts (and what is then extrapolated out to the subtypes). It's been my goal throughout this book to share the most useful and practical information possible, and

I believe understanding the instincts to be invaluable. Once again, there are many approaches to working with the instincts and subtypes, and there is little consensus even among master teachers on which way is the right way. I'm sharing with you what I have found to be the most helpful, valuable, and actionable information on the instincts and subtypes.

Aside from our core types, all people have developed three Instinctual Drives that are located in the Body Center. These instincts are often deeply unconscious but are vital to our survival both individually and as a species. Similar to how we develop dominant and repressed Centers of Intelligence, we will be hyperfocused on one instinct and leave one as a blind spot. Our dominant instinct is what determines our subtype. According to the Narrative Enneagram, the dominant instinct is where we discharge the energy of our Emotional Habit, thus varying the "look and feel" of a type based on which instinct is dominant. And just like our Centers of Intelligence, we need to develop healthy, lifegiving expressions of our instincts and find balance among them in order to further our personal and spiritual growth. As we become more aware of these unconscious habits, the energy that is normally discharged through the instincts becomes the fuel for spiritual transformation.

Self-preservation (self-prez, or SP): This instinct has everything to do with our own physical survival. It's concerned with having "enough" for a satisfactory survival. It focuses on security, the home and immediate family, work as a means of generating income, and our own personal appetites. When functioning properly, the self-preservation instinct creates a warm and safe place for us all to gather (literally or metaphorically), and there is a sense of abundance that creates feelings of safety and calm. The self-prez instinct helps us treat everyone like family. When the instinct is distorted or overused, it can lead to anxiety, a privileged or "me first" attitude, or a dauntless or even reckless pursuit of financial or material possessions. People with a dominant SP instinct are often described as warm and can be the more introverted and anxious variant of their type, choosing to stay close to home more often than going out and adventuring. Often the self-prez instinct can cause people to overfocus on their work, becoming workaholics in order to ensure that they are providing enough for themselves and for their family.

Sexual (one-to-one, or SX): The sexual instinct, which is sometimes called the one-to-one instinct, is about our sexuality and sexual drive—but more than just that, it's also knowing ourselves through intimate, one-on-one relationships as well as our connection to and expression of our own creative impulse. When functioning properly, the sexual instinct generates passion between people, for personal projects, and for spiritual endeavors. People with a dominant sexual instinct have a certain heat and intensity about them. They tend to exhibit strength and beauty and can be seductive or even aggressive. These are also people who may be more highly concerned with where they fall in the masculinity/femininity continuum. Sexual instinct dominance usually leads people to seek a kind of union with another person, be it romantically, sexually, or just as a friend. This drive can also cause people to become jealous or possessive of their people and highly competitive for their attention. They want to hold all of what another person will give them in a sort of sacred confidentiality. The sexual instinct can drive a certain fascination with other people as well as projects or interests. These people are more easily absorbed by their interests and work projects but in a way that is distinctly more intense than their self-prez counterparts.

Social (SO): The social instinct is what keeps us attuned to how we are doing in our community. It is focused on the good of the group over the individual and seeks to bring people together and keep people connected. People who have a dominant social instinct are more focused on how they fit into their groups and how their groups are doing. They have a strong desire for participation in something bigger than themselves. These types can be more wrapped up in what others think of them, possibly showing more ambition or more blatantly seeking prestige. They can easily fall into the shame/honor dichotomy, depending on how others view them. These people often work for social causes and place a high value on friendship. They will sacrifice or limit themselves in order to fulfill their duty to the group. When this instinct is functioning properly, it helps us find meaning and purpose in our communities and allows us to stay more connected to those around us. When this instinct is distorted, there is a tendency to either avoid communities completely or to hyperfocus on the community to the detriment of its members. This can create a cult-like energy in groups.

THE THREE-LEGGED STOOL
. . . .

A considerable and direct connection exists between our Instinctual Drives and the three-legged stool of practice, lineage, and community that we've discussed throughout this book. The Instinctual Drives are the ways in which each of us seek to find fulfillment and meaning in our lives; they are the ways the life force or spirit flow through us. They can be developed and life-giving or distorted and underdeveloped. As I discussed, the Instinctual Drives, much like our three centers, can be over- or underdeveloped because of a hyper- or hypo-focus on them, and a large part of our growth and development as a person depends on our ability to access each of these instincts at the appropriate time. When all three Instinctual Drives are operating fully and in a balanced way, we can feel the flow of life and spirit moving through us in a way that is enriching and fulfilling. The self-preservation or self-prez instinct oversees our personal security through physical safety, material possessions, the rhythms and routines of everyday life, and immediate family relations. This instinct is directly related to the leg of our personal practices. The sexual or one-to-one instinct is concerned with the creative impulse in all of its forms and oversees issues of sex, sexuality, intimacy, and close relationships as well as our connection to the divine, our creative expression, and the intensity and vitality of the energy in our bodies. This instinct is directly related to our lineage. The social instinct oversees our place in our group or society, ideas of belonging and participation in something bigger than ourselves, and understanding and navigating social structures. This instinct is directly related to the leg of community in our personal work.

RESOURCES

• •

My hope is that this book has provided both a strong foundation of Enneagram knowledge as well as actionable steps for how to move into the work that the Enneagram is inviting us into. That being said, there is no way I could possibly share everything there is to know about the Enneagram in one book, and I am fully aware of my particular bias in sharing what I've shared. If you've found this tool captivating, I strongly encourage you to continue your study not just with my work but with the work of as many qualified and experienced Enneagram teachers as you can find. Here is a list of my favorites:

Schools

The Narrative Enneagram, founded by Helen Palmer and Dr. David Daniels: http://www.enneagramworldwide.com

The Enneagram Institute, founded by Don Riso and Russ Hudson: http://www.theenneagraminstitute.com

Teachers

Marion Gilbert—http://www.mariongilbert.com

Terry Saracino—https://enneagramworldwide.com/teachers/terry/

Renée Rosario—https://www.enneasight.com

Peter O'Hanrahan—http://www.theenneagramatwork.com

Chichi Agorom—http://www.thisspaceco.com

Evan Barbee—http://www.evanbarbee.com

Sarah Duet—http://www.sarahduet.com

Organizations

The International Enneagram Association—https://www.internationalenneagram.org

Enneagram in Color—http://www.instagram.com/enneagramincolor/
Queer Enneagram—http://www.queerenneagram.com

Books

The Enneagram: Understanding Yourself and the Others in Your Life, Helen Palmer

The Modern Enneagram: Discover Who You Are and Who You Can Be, Kacie Berghoef and Melanie Bell

The Wisdom of the Enneagram: The Complete Guide to Psychological and Spiritual Growth for the Nine Personality Types, Don Richard Riso and Russ Hudson

The Enneagram in Love and Work: Understanding Your Intimate and Business Relationships, Helen Palmer